FREEDOM
Nationally
VIRTUE
Locally
Or
SOCIALISM

KEVIN MILLER

Denali Press
A Division of MT6 Media, Inc.

DENALI
PRESS

Denali Press
A Division of MT6 Media, Inc.

5445 DTC Parkway
Penthouse Four
Greenwood Village, Colorado 80111

ISBN: 978-0-615-40039-6

Printed in the United States

This book will please no one except those millions of Americans who stubbornly cling to the belief that they, their children, and their grandchildren should be a free people, a people who—apart from the Federal Government—freely choose their own virtues.

> "I know of no safe depository of the ultimate powers of the society but the people themselves; and if we think them not enlightened enough to exercise their control with a wholesome discretion, the remedy is not to take it from them, but to inform their discretion."
>
> Thomas Jefferson

To Cathy, Travis, and Alexis,
each and all gifts bringing great joy

ACKNOWLEDGEMENTS

Many heartfelt thanks are due.

This project simply would have never happened without Debbie Brown's encouragement over a year ago. Larry Heinrich threw his influence and enthusiasm behind it. Thom Scheffel was a vital encouragement and valued colleague from well before the beginning. And the many attendees at Vanguard Roundtable over the years have been the iron that sharpens.

Troy Reichert jump-started the reality of publishing this book. Bob Grizzle and Ken Larson of Denali Press had the vision from the beginning. Utilizing his extensive experience and fresh passion, Les Middleton guided astutely. Becky Fox was ever gracious and effective in her editing role. Robin Crosslin contributed his creative insight. The criticisms, thoughts, comments, and suggestions of many other colleagues and friends in various forums were deeply appreciated.

Cathy Miller was as supportive and essential as ever and is simply the best blessing one could ever hope for, well beyond a single project.

Of course, opinions expressed in this book are not necessarily shared by these generous people.

Soli Deo Gloria.

Kevin Miller
October 2010
Aurora, Colorado

CONTENTS

PREFACE
GOT SOCIALISM?

This short book was written entirely with someone like you in mind.

Someone too busy to read something that doesn't directly impact work or family. Someone too busy to dive into politics, and public policy, and the Constitution, and freedom, and virtue. You shouldn't have to. You're busy raising kids. Serving people well at work. Helping build a business. Paying the mortgage. Saving for retirement. Volunteering at the local food bank.

That's why you vote—you're busy with life and you've been trusting that common sense and solid principles would ultimately prevail in the nation's capital. Yeah, sure, it could happen—with a little give and take, a little pork barrel, a little inefficiency, a little waste. After all, the Federal Government runs the post office, what do you expect?

But something bigger, much bigger, has been forced on you and your neighbors. The craziness of what-in-the-world's-happening-to-our-freedom has literally grabbed your attention. You know, the freedom you had when you grew up, now evaporating for your kids and grandkids because of all the changes taking place.

As part of that Federal power-grab by the most powerful government in the world, you see new "virtues" being created every day, agendas crammed down by people who have never even been to your community and who don't really care about your values and your freedom.

Agendas where nameless, faceless, unaccountable bureaucrats have decided countless times how you and about three hundred million others are going to live.

And, adding insult to injury, agendas that you will have to pay for with more taxes.

These agendas are really just socialism. But they are two types of socialism, both "economic-socialism," where the goal is the redistribution of wealth by the government, and "virtue-socialism," where the goal is to ratchet the entire country's behavior to a deadly serious political-correctness in all areas of culture and life.

That political correctness was originally interpreted as harmless foolishness by many Americans, but it's a grim business now. The Federal Government's wealth redistribution and cram-down of secular "virtues" in America is being accomplished by force of law and regulation.

Deeply concerned? You should be. We all should be.

But there's a completely different path to take.

A straightforward path.

A path that was conceived and hammered out over 200 years ago, an approach that was further refined in the decades following.

A path that's not kooky or on the fringe of what tens of millions of Americans think and know from hard-fought experience.

A path that's the only clear path to America's greatness.

That path is "freedom nationally, virtue locally."

Read this short, easy-to-read book, and then pass it on. It could change your children's lives. And it may even succeed quickly enough to change yours.

CHAPTER 1

THE SLOW BUT SURE ROUTE TO DESTRUCTION

When Americans Ask the Federal Government to Deliver Both Freedom and Virtue, They Will Get Neither

> "It is true that liberty is precious—
> so precious that it must be rationed."
> Vladmir Lenin, Russian revolutionary,
> attributed by Sidney and Beatrice Webb[1]

Two stories are happening at the same time. First, Americans enjoy an extraordinary heritage of freedom: economic freedom, religious liberty, and freedom to choose their own personal values. Second, Americans are rapidly losing these very freedoms.

The second story, of precious freedom lost, will prevail unless Americans change the way their Federal Government works.

Here are just a few examples of the typical nonsense coming out of Washington.

Americans are Choosing the "Wrong" Light Bulbs, Every Day

Thomas Edison perfected the incandescent light bulb long ago. You know, that simple little bulb that you use virtually everywhere. High-priced marketplace alternatives to that low-cost bulb already exist; yet, the first choice, by far, of many Americans is this low-cost, high-value delivery of light.

But the all-wise Federal Government has declared that this extraordinary invention, useful for decades, is unacceptable. Too much energy used, you see.

According to the Federal Government, buyers of light bulbs in millions of private homes have not been energy-preservation-conscious-enough, not green enough—therefore, not virtuous enough—so the sale of these handy and economical bulbs in America is scheduled to become illegal, beginning in 2012.

Powerful Federal Bureaucrats Choose Fish Over People

In late 2008, the U.S. Fish and Wildlife Service decided to divert billions of gallons of water during the next year from farmers in the fertile San Joaquin Valley, an area very much dependent economically on necessary water. Why the water diversion? The delta smelt fish, a two-inch-long fish that is one of many species of fish in the area that are protected by the Endangered Species Act, was determined by the Federal Government to be in special peril.

The Federal Government's understanding of virtue in this case, as decided by an unelected bureaucracy, required the choosing of the delta smelt fish over the opportunity of farmers to access irrigation water and over the gainful employment of farm employees.

But a key California Department of Water Resources official later indicated that the Federal Government's biological opinion could be overstating the threat because the delta smelt existed elsewhere.[2] After that, U.S. District Judge Oliver W. Wanger issued a ruling on the delta smelt issue. *The Fresno Bee* reported on June 23, 2010 that "Wanger's ruling found that water officials must consider humans along with the smelt in limiting use of the delta for irrigation and urban use. The judge also found that water users made convincing arguments that the federal government's science didn't prove that increased pumping [of water] from the delta imperiled the smelt." As of late June 2010, a compromise was reached where a certain amount of water could be pumped, but not amounts above the biological opinion issued by the Federal Government.[3]

In the meantime, the San Joaquin Valley was devastated economically during 2009 as the water shortages took their human toll.

By force of bureaucratic power, Washington-decided "virtues" trumped local virtues during a time crucial to thousands of local Californians.

Americans Are Forced to Buy Health Coverage

In 2010, the U.S. President and the United States Congress legislated that the purchase of health coverage will be compulsory for every American. That's because, the President said, that's "the right thing to do."[4]

The highly conceited presumption is that the President and Congress know virtue better than ordinary Americans. So, they are ready not just to instruct Americans about virtue, they are actually going to <u>force every American to be virtuous</u>.

So, when a young, healthy, single 27-year-old entrepreneur wants to prioritize hiring workers and purchasing job-creating inventory over purchasing her personal health insurance, she apparently isn't virtuous enough to understand how to deploy her own scarce resources. Instead, the Federal Government *needs* to specifically tell that citizen how to prioritize her own finances.

The Federal virtue-cram-down machine spoke from the mountaintop. The new law will be applied to individuals in significantly different circumstances in every nook and cranny of a very large and complex nation. Every adult American *will* purchase health coverage.

Of course, this legislation is simply a massive, <u>forced reprioritization</u> by the Federal Government of <u>individual Americans' private budgeting and decision-making</u>.

Virtue Cram-Downs by the Federal Government

These are just three examples of Federal virtue cram-downs, among the multitudes that ordinary Americans actually experience every day in an up-close and personal way.

The reality is crystal clear to millions of Americans on the receiving end of countless Federal virtue cram-downs. Americans are routinely losing their basic freedoms. Ironically, they are losing these freedoms to the unchecked whims and wishes of the very people they are paying to serve them.

The Constant Race to Win at Virtue-Politics

Pretty much all people in America say that they are for freedom. And they sincerely are! They are for their own particular brand of freedom, but, because they are human, they want limitations on others.

This is totally understandable when an entrepreneur wants to run a strip club next to your daughter's elementary school, and hundreds of local tax-paying families object. After all, that entrepreneur can build his enterprise elsewhere.

It is significantly less understandable when federal employees, hired and paid to serve the entire country, decide what type of light bulbs Americans *in the entire country* can buy, decide what Federal-Government-approved low-fat or low-salt foods *all* Americans might eat, and decide that the delta smelt fish is more important than the livelihood of thousands of Americans.

Secularists may call them "values," Christians may call them "virtues," and each group thinks its belief set is superior to the other's. But whatever they are called, these are the deep passions of the politically-engaged. Some are high-minded passions, some very much less so—whichever they are, they are driving the current political scene in America.

Regardless of the label, these passions simply *must* be fulfilled, you see, because the entire country supposedly would be better off. This is the rising secular theocracy, where those in power in the gargantuan Federal Government horse-trade their way to codifying into law and enforcing every "virtue" imaginable—and many "virtues" unimaginable.

So, why aim small, at families, or communities, or churches, where true and accurate common interest can be locally determined? Why simply work to improve local organizations when the entire country could be so deeply "virtuous" in so many ways? You know: "virtue," a particular rule that you want 300 million people to obey, and fund with their own hard-earned money.

Therefore, the nation's highest-elected leaders vigorously engage in virtue-politics. Forcing educational standards on the uninterested, fighting a "war" on poverty, rescuing the always-precarious plight of favored animals—nothing escapes the attention of the federal-virtue eyes-of-the-beholders.

Everybody "Important" in Washington Gets Their Turn

The growth of the Federal Government in Washington is achieved through virtue-politics. The old reliable issues that require Washington's attention, such as national defense and ho-hum established entitlements, well, that's so *yesterday*.

So, the Federal Government never really totally blocks any one particular virtue-agenda, because Federal virtue-agendas grow the Federal Government. Oh, there are very strong fights among competing agendas. Yes, some agendas lose here and there, but the virtue-cram-down machine never stops churning out new laws and new regulations.

Sooner or later, no one important in Washington is denied his or her turn at the magical virtue-cram-down steering wheel. They are all people-pleasers, fully dedicated to pleasing the countless campaign-funding special interests, the brand-new-Federal-project-here home-towners, the merit-leveling crusaders for equal outcomes and "social justice," and the entitlement-grabbing moralists. The list of constituents is endless, and endlessly gratifying to the "public servant."

In this way, year after year, decade after decade, the unapologetic culture of the Federal virtue cram-down has developed and thrived.

In one political party's Federal administration, it's about deeper federal attention to religious outreaches and deeper federal involvement in education, supposedly with an expected result of "no child left behind."

Then the other political party's Federal administration gets elected. To them, it's about comprehensive Federal involvement in all Americans' personal health choices, and it's about making Chevrolets, moving beyond merely extensive regulations required of a giant auto company to actual ownership of the company itself.

Always, it's done in the name of the "crisis" of the day, and it's done in the name of the virtue being applied. No "crisis" passes without newly-legislated "progress." Apparently, religious outreaches, *and* local schools, *and* the auto industry, *and* even any one individual American without health coverage—*and* whatever else strikes Washington's fancy—cannot possibly thrive without Federal virtue-cramdowns. Ultimately, every conceivable organization and every American are targeted, often multiple times.

The Virtue-Cram-Down Culture Unrelentingly Reduces Freedom

These virtue cram-downs are often led by individuals sworn to uphold the U.S. Constitution. Apparently, however, these people are not always focused on whether their actions are Constitutional. Instead, they are primarily focused on "improving" the lives of Americans by their compliance to brand new "virtues." And with every Federal virtue cram-down, freedom is reduced.

A particular political culture has developed in Washington. It takes just one of 535 legislators—or just one of a million or so unaccountable-to-the-electorate, Federal-employee bureaucrats—to fulfill his or her highly-coveted place in history by determining and enforcing a newly-discovered virtue that is *absolutely necessary* for ordinary Americans.

So, numerous, influential Washington-attracted individuals work to fulfill their destiny of creating a Totally Virtuous

America. They are busy as beavers, constantly cramming-down new virtues and installing more new requirements, in order to serve their special-interest-of-vital-importance-today-that-we-must-not-neglect.

Each time, it's just a small "virtue" needed, you see. But that "virtue" is vastly important to the future of the world, or to the animal kingdom, or to a financially-contributing constituent, or to a future employer, or even to Western civilization or its recent replacement, multiculturalism. And, every "virtue" is important enough to force every American to comply with new Federal rules, of course.

These federal employees, elected and unelected, defy easy categorization. They can be Democrat, Republican, Christian, Jew, atheist, male, female, straight, gay, Congress-person, judge, or bureaucrat. Each plays a part in defining and shaping the behavior of 300 million Americans.

In this way, an iron-fisted set of "virtues" is forged by a supposedly-competing coalition of interests: atheist and Christian, urban and rural, New York and West Virginia, General Motors and Chrysler, Goldman Sachs and AIG. And these virtues are enforced by the ever-willing, ever-expand-ing bureaucracy.

Sure, there are a few federal employees, elected or unelected, opposing this agenda. But somehow they rarely seem to truly prevail for the truly common interest.

And multitudes of Americans are quite happy, if not jubilant, to get their direct, special-interest need filled or personally-emotional pet virtue codified and enforced by the U.S. Federal Government. The Federal Government, the most powerful government in the history of the world, relishes controlling every detail.

The Federal Government Cannot Deliver Both Freedom and Virtue

But the result to the common interests of ordinary Americans is inevitable.

When Americans ask the Federal Government to deliver both freedom and virtue, they will ultimately get neither.

Here that is again.

When Americans ask the Federal Government to deliver both freedom and virtue, they will ultimately get neither.

There are at least three reasons this is true.

First, 535 legislators cannot possibly properly define virtues for all Americans to live by. This is true in the best of circumstances, let alone in the current era where significant moral confusion is the rule. But, no matter the era, the U.S. Congress is not structurally designed to create a set of timeless virtues via the inherently messy legislative process.

To the contrary, real virtue is clear. Real virtue comes as a clarion call of clear-sighted conscience and conviction to individuals, not from a group-grope of literally hundreds of politicians. These politicians, some of whom are quite ethically-challenged anyway, are focused on securing compromises in order to pass legislation, getting reelected every election cycle, serving very dissimilar constituents, and pleasing self-interested financial supporters.

Has the multitude of Federal laws, say, in the last forty years, fostered real, true-blue virtue in America? Some good intentions were in evidence, certainly. Bad intentions were evident, too, to be certain! But virtue? No, to the extent virtue is to be had, Americans are virtuous *in spite of* Washington, not because of Washington.

Second, a million or so often-entrenched, unaccountable government bureaucrats cannot possibly deliver virtue. The public-sector employees charged with implementation of Federal legislation cannot possibly deliver even the best-intended virtue commanded by Federal legislation.

At best, the bureaucrats might occasionally deliver some measure of outward, visible compliance with Federal rules. At worst, they pile on even more burdensome requirements, with pages upon pages of rules that require costly compliance. For goodness sake, the United States Postal Service does not efficiently deliver a letter from location A to location B.

No, virtue is not something forced from above by a federal government. It never has been. The idea of virtue being created and delivered by a federal government is simply laughable. Rules, yes. Virtue, no.

Third, every Federal virtue cram-down reduces the freedom of Americans in some measure. And the total of all the Federal virtue cram-downs reduce freedom in large measure.

That measure of freedom lost is in the replacement of local values with Federal Government rules and requirements, the precious time and effort routinely wasted dealing with Federal Government directives and reporting, increased taxes, increased costs for ordinary goods, and reductions in daily choices for many Americans. Unfortunately, many

Americans have come to understand that these are the very goals of many of the people, elected or unelected, who are cramming-down Federal Government virtues.

Journalism morphed in recent decades from the goal of reporting the news to the goal of changing the world. Unfortunately, similar to journalism, government service in key seats of power has supposedly matured, too. Far from serving all the people, government service is often targeted to a particular, specialized agenda, a *necessary* set of virtues, at the always-worth-it-expense-and-sacrifice-of-everybody-else.

Also, the huge behemoth that is the Federal Government cannot possibly be a good steward of the vast resources—the tax monies—entrusted to it. Every American has a different story of bad government stewardship. Unfortunately, that's because there are so many to choose from.

And these Federal virtue cram-downs accumulate, weakening the nation in vital ways.

★ *Federal virtue cram-downs inherently pit Americans one against another*, forcing many to serve the special interests of a few.

This is true in the income tax code. It is true in special interest legislation. It is true with earmarks. And it is true with regard to virtually every piece of virtue legislation departing Congress.

★ *True justice gets thwarted, and citizen cynicism abounds.* That's because even seemingly good intentions go awry (e.g., the Federal Government's so-called War on Poverty worked to destroy many families).

★ The *huge economic costs* of Federal-virtue-cram-down programs and regulations reduce the competitiveness of American companies in world markets, hamper job-creation, and hamstring vital entrepreneurship crucial to American prosperity.

★ *Real, voluntary virtues* (e.g., *effectively* helping neighbors) *are replaced by fake, coerced virtues* (e.g., every American's use of the "correct" light bulbs).

Is It a New Thing for Virtue Cram-Downs to Diminish Freedom?

Simply put, freedom is reduced with every Federal virtue cram-down.

Often it is the freedom of someone specific, such as the farm employees left unemployed in the economically-devastated San Joaquin Valley. Of course, they were left with plenty of time to gaze at the french-fry-sized delta smelt fish to blame for putting them out of work. Often, it is *all* the American people who have their virtues redefined, their choices reduced, and their tax burdens increased by these Federal-Government-enforced "virtues."

Surely, this is a new thing, right?

CHAPTER 2

THE UNEXPECTED GIFT IN THE 1780s

The Rapid Blooming of American Patriots' Overbearing Government

> "I know of no safe depository of the ultimate powers of the society but the people themselves; and if we think them not enlightened enough to exercise their control with a wholesome discretion, the remedy is not to take it from them, but to inform their discretion."
>
> Thomas Jefferson, in a letter to William Charles Jarvis in 1820[5]

The most important fifteen years of political history for Americans—and, for that matter, many hundreds of millions of people experiencing freedom today—was the period 1776 to 1791.

And it was about the first fifteen years of *American* history because so much in America, and ultimately in many other countries around the world, was impacted by this critical period in the United States.

The Declaration, the War, and the Articles of Confederation

First, of course, were the Declaration of Independence and the resulting Revolutionary War. Many in the English colonies had tired of the policies of King George and the British Parliament. Governance seemed remote while taxes levied seemed oppressive. While a number of people were sympathetic to the Crown, the move for independence from Britain won the day.

The Second Continental Congress had appointed a committee to draft a constitution. That Congress took some months to finally agree to the Articles of Confederation in 1777. And, in March 1781, the Articles of Confederation went into effect with their ratification by the state of Maryland. So, between the time of Declaration of Independence and the ratification of the Articles, the fledgling country had survived without benefit of a formal centralizing document, relying on the leadership and the generosity of key Patriots.

Later in 1781, the British surrendered at Yorktown and a new nation had finally secured its independence. But there was much for the young nation and the states to learn.

The Articles of Confederation, agreed to by Americans generally wary of national government, had grave weaknesses and were inadequate to the needs of a young nation. Under the Articles, for example, a unicameral legislature meant there was no separation of powers; the national legislature could not tax to meet the financial needs of the nation, including paying the nation's debts; and amending the Articles required almost-impossible unanimity by all states.

Overbearing Government in America in the 1780s

In the meantime, various states' leaders went wild. In his memoir, *Recovering the Past: A Historian's Memoir*, eminent Constitutional-era historian Forrest McDonald crisply summarizes pre-U.S. Constitution 1780s governance this way:

> . . . The bumbling and ineffectual way in which Congress managed [under the Articles of Confederation] is fairly well known.
>
> What the real governments of the several United States were doing is less well known. They were oppressing American citizens under a burden of taxation and regulation greater than any they had ever experienced, greater than any that had been coveted by the wickedest minister who had ever advised the British Crown.
>
> The level of taxes during the 1780s was ten to twenty times prewar norms, and the increase in the volume of legislation, despite ostensible constitutional checks on the legislative power, dwarfed the increase in taxes.
>
> Quite in addition to the wholesale wartime persecution of those who remained loyal to England, legislation was enacted to regulate what people could produce and sell and what they could charge for it;
>
> to interfere systematically with private commercial transactions and suspend the obligations of private contracts;
>
> to prohibit the purchase of luxuries, prescribe what people could eat or drink, and govern what they could wear;

to regulate private morality, indoctrinate the citizens with official dogmas, and suppress contrary opinions;

to inflate the currency deliberately to pay for the ever-mounting costs of government. All this and more was imposed upon a people so unaccustomed to taxation that they had been willing to rebel against their king rather than submit to even nominal taxes levied by Parliament; so unaccustomed to governmental intrusion upon their private lives as to be willing to fight and die to preserve their personal liberties; and so conservative that they could perceive the encroachments of Crown and Parliament only as violations of the ancient constitution. . . .

Thus it was that, though we usually think of the Constitution as having been designed to overcome the weaknesses of the Articles of Confederation by establishing new power, the vast majority of the Framers viewed the crises of 1787 as having arisen from an excess of state government, a wanton and inept use of all government power, and a collapse of authority resulting from efforts to overgovern much.[6] (emphasis mine and paragraph separations mine)

Understandably, many of the infant nation's leaders were dismayed at the condition of governance, with a structurally inadequate Federal Government and several quite overbearing state governments. What independence from Britain seemed to have wrought was something worse than the administration of King George himself!

The problem of coercive, overreaching power being exercised was no longer that of a remote king. Now, the problem was some of Americans' actual friends and neighbors.

Key American Leaders' Reactions in the 1780s

Needless to say, many who had pledged "[their] lives, [their] fortunes, [their] sacred honor" in the Declaration of Independence were not pleased. They had paid a huge price for freedom, and the overbearing government and politics of the day did not set well with many.

George Washington, leader of the victorious Continental Army and later the first President of the United States, corresponded with friends about his amazement at the poor governance he observed.

James Madison, later the fifth President of the United States and known as the Father of the Constitution, complained both about the lack of wisdom in the many laws being passed and about the volume of legislation passed in just a few years exceeding that of the previous century.

Thomas Jefferson, later the third President of the United States, was also deeply concerned about state governments' tendency towards despotism. His famous observation was, "173 despots would surely be as oppressive as one . . . An *elective despotism* was not the government we fought for."[7]

An amusing point is that *The Patriot,* the entertaining movie about the Revolutionary War, has a similar line about local despots. The movie character, Benjamin Martin, played by actor Mel Gibson, said, "Would you tell me please, Mr. Howard, why should I trade one tyrant three thousand miles away for three thousand tyrants one mile away? An elected legislature can trample a man's rights as easily as a king can."[8]

However, that movie line is spoken during the beginning of the War. Jefferson, grounded in later first-hand reality, published his observation about an elective despotism in 1785, nearly a decade after the Declaration of Independence.

Washington, Jefferson, Madison—these leaders were not radicals. But it wasn't supposed to have happened this way, of course. John Adams, later to become the second President of the United States, held the opinion in 1776 that a "democratic despotism" was a contradiction in terms. But a democratic despotism of overbearing state governments *did* happen, in short order.

By this time, King George must have been highly amused as he witnessed many Americans descend into oppressive governance far more onerous than anything that Britain had installed. "Give me liberty or give me death," the rallying cry coined by Patrick Henry, must have been ringing in King George's ears!

Overbearing Government Actually an Unexpected Gift

Clearly, the first efforts of the Americans had substantially failed at both the federal and the state levels.

Yet, in retrospect, the irony is that a decade's worth of the dramatic failure of governance structure and overbearing office-holding were probably just what the infant nation needed.

Suppose the Articles of Confederation and all the state governments had been at least somewhat closer to fostering reasonable governance. If so, the United States of America might well have limped along for some years, entrenching bad structures and bad leadership as acceptable.

As it was, however, key leaders in the young nation understood that the very foundation they had fought for—freedom and self-determination for every American—was at stake. Had the various state governments been reasonable, not overbearing, perhaps there would have been no perceived need for a new Constitution.

But, just what should the young nation do, specifically, in response to the inadequacy of the Articles of Confederation, and in response to the startlingly overbearing governance of the 1780s in some states?

CHAPTER 3

A YOUNG NATION GETS ANCHORED FOR POSSIBLE GREATNESS

The Amazing Story of Five Years in the Life of James Madison

"A republic, if you can keep it."
Benjamin Franklin, answering a question about
what the Constitution's Framers had produced[9]

 B ut, just what should the young nation do, specifically, in response to the inadequacy of the Articles of Confederation, and in response to the startlingly overbearing governance of the 1780s in some states?

The answer about what to do began with the Constitutional Convention in Philadelphia. Understanding the key parts of that answer is very important for freedom-cherishing Americans today.

Convention Attendees' Actual First-Hand Experience Is Crucial

At least four factors were crucial at the Convention.

First, the attendees were educated by their firsthand experiences with King George and the British Parliament.

Second, the Articles of Confederation then in place were inadequate for the nation.

Third, key state governments in the just-preceding years in the 1780s were overbearing.

And, fourth, key attendees were surely disappointed in their own previously-held, faulty judgment that self-government in America would presumptively be filled to the brim with the freedom that the Patriots had fought for.

These areas of deficiency in others and in themselves, were crucial to developing a strong Constitution. The attendees coupled that knowledge with a keen understanding of human nature and deep study of the history of republics of the past. The result was the creation of the most profound governance philosophy and document in history, before or since.

James Madison was one of the Founders at the very center of the action. Madison has been called the Father of the Constitution. While the delegates to the Convention "wrote" the Constitution, his Virginia Plan is widely regarded as the model actually used as the starting point for the drafting of the U.S. Constitution. But the path by which the Constitution was embraced and ratified was not very direct.

Federalists and Anti-Federalists

Leaders of the time reached different conclusions about what primary lessons should be drawn from the experiences of the last dozen or so years.

These leaders broke roughly into two groups, the Federalists and the Anti-Federalists. There were many issues, but key debates encompassed, first, whether the national government would have too much power; second, whether a national bill of rights was necessary; and, third, whether a republican government could serve such a broad constituency in a large republic well.

The Convention unfolded with representatives from twelve states attending; Rhode Island did not send representatives. Soon, it was clear that the generally Federalist position had the defining hand in the drafting, with the necessity of a stronger central government considered key.

Some Founders believed that state governments had performed badly because of the rather low caliber of elected state representatives. This apparently condescending attitude about the quality of state leadership helped drive some Anti-Federalists to believe that the nation's governing elite under a new constitution would do just that—govern elitely, with little regard for the average American's rights.

With this deep-seated belief that *every* national government would not hesitate to trample the rights of citizens, the Anti-Federalists remained highly concerned about the lack of a national bill of rights.

George Mason had written part of the Virginia Declaration of Rights, which stated "that all men are by nature equally free and independent, and have certain inherent rights" and "that all power is vested in, and consequently derived from, the people; that magistrates are their trustees and servants, and at all times amenable to them." The

Virginia Declaration got specific about many rights, from freedom of the press, to the right to a speedy trial, to the right not to self-incriminate—to name just three.[10]

Other states paralleled Virginia with their own bills of rights. These documents varied, yet held to the same basic idea: namely, individuals' rights existed independent of and properly free of interference by the State.

Constitutional Convention Results and Aftermath

The Federalists generally won the day, creating in the Constitution a much stronger national government than the Articles of Confederation afforded. The Constitution enumerated specific powers of government and created three branches of government, with checks and balances designed right in.

Key Federalists—Alexander Hamilton, John Jay, and James Madison—swung into action immediately. Their goal was to garner support from the American people by writing a convincing series of articles for newspaper publication in New York, later published as *The Federalist* or *The Federalist Papers*.

But the Anti-Federalists remained deeply dissatisfied. Key leaders of the faction included Patrick Henry, George Mason, and George Clinton. Many Americans strongly shared their concerns.

Even though Thomas Jefferson was remotely located in Europe as minister to France, his sentiments clearly lay with a national bill of rights.

Running for Congress in a Virginia district with a large number of Anti-Federalists, the Federalist James Madison pledged to work for the adoption of a national bill of rights.

When Madison was elected, the Federalists in Congress were not inclined to address the issue of a national bill of rights. But Madison persevered, winnowing dozens of amendments proposed by state ratifying conventions down to a handful.

Madison didn't stop there; he took up the cause of the Bill of Rights in his speeches. This was a principled stand taken, reconsidered and deliberated upon by a man who as a Federalist had offered many arguments against what he now pursued. And he did that now in the face of his colleagues who encouraged him to jettison his integrity and forego his promise.

How far removed Madison's principled stand and ethical framework seem from the vast majority of elected officials today! Surely, Madison's pledge regarding a national bill of rights was one of the most important political promises ever made and then actually kept in the history of America.

The Dramatic Difference Made by One Man

Early on, many Federalists had maintained that a bill of rights wasn't needed, because the government was not empowered in the Constitution to violate the "natural rights" that were ultimately spelled out in the Bill of Rights. In other words, Federalists typically asserted that government would routinely respect all those individual rights that the government was not empowered to intrude upon.

The Anti-Federalists maintained that this great experiment in self-government required that key rights for Americans be spelled out. Why? They studied history, they had experienced King George from England, and they had also experienced the miniature King Georges that some of their key state leaders had become in the 1780s.

Besides, the U.S. Constitution was really the first such document of its kind. Given the track record of all governments in world history, why would the American Federal Government be fully trustworthy with unwritten promises?

Historians' debates might center around whether the Bill of Rights was actually needed. For example, one issue might be whether individual Americans would have had their rights preserved without a written and ratified Bill of Rights. Another issue might be whether that preservation of individual rights would be sustained for over two centuries.

But one thing seems very clear. The Anti-Federalists got the essence of human nature right—powerful, unchecked government officials will invariably trample individual rights with impunity, under a variety of guises.

The Bill of Rights was ratified by the necessary number of states by December 15, 1791. The Constitution, as amended by the Bill of Rights, was complete.

So, Madison, a key Federalist, kept his promise and actually became a crucial factor in the crafting and ratification of the Bill of Rights, an Anti-Federalist position. His leadership in a short five years helped bring the Constitution into a profound and necessary permanent embrace of both individual rights and a strong national government needed for the nation's defense.

The Constitution, even with its flaws, became the extraordinary, foundational-yet-flexible document that would accommodate the inherently-necessary granting or expansions of freedom for all Americans (i.e., African-Americans, Native Americans, and women).

The most important fifteen years in modern political history had drawn to a close.

But the last five years of that span were truly extraordinary. During that time, the thoughtful leadership of James Madison helped bring both the Federalist and the Anti-Federalist positions to fruition. He was instrumental in helping the young nation avoid any tipping-point dissatisfaction with national governance, where all might be lost, such as a possible second Constitutional convention. And he led in creating the crucial anchor for a young nation to pursue greatness.

Madison, with his co-Framers of the Constitution, had forged a remarkable structure of a federal government responsible for "freedom nationally," with "virtue locally" reserved to the people and their local structures.

While Federal office holders were to discharge their limited, spelled-out responsibilities virtuously and for the public good (it was hoped), the Constitutional Amendments in the Bill of Rights were designed, among other things, to assure Americans that citizens' virtues themselves (e.g., religious beliefs) would not be defined by the Federal Government.

CHAPTER 4

JUST WHO IS CAESAR?
The Breakthrough

> "The Americans are the first people whom Heaven has favored
> with an opportunity of deliberating upon and choosing
> the forms of government under which they should live."
>
> John Jay, the first Chief Justice
> of the Supreme Court of the United States[II]

One of the most famous teachings of Jesus Christ is to render to Caesar the things that are Caesar's, and to God the things that are God's.

But, first things first.

The actual question faced by Americans on July 5, 1776—the morning after the Declaration of Independence—and the years immediately following was, just who is "Caesar"?

First, Real-World Experience Spoke

While it might not have been clear exactly what they did want, Founding-era Americans came to certain conclusions about their current realities, deficiencies, or problems. Here's a short list.

★ No replacement for the <u>sovereign office</u> of King George, thank you. Even with the highly impressive George Washington as a fairly presumptive candidate, there was no broad and enduring sentiment for an American monarchy.

★ The Declaration of Independence, key to the founding of America and lofty in language, did not definitively establish who Caesar was or should be.

★ The Articles of Confederation, combined with the various state governments, really comprised the first American attempt at defining who Caesar would be. As we have seen, the results were dismal, even alarming, to key leaders.

The fifteen years of real-world experience between 1776 and 1791 without an effective Caesar were essential to the forging of the American understanding of Caesar in America.

Second, Learned Education
Leavened with Common Sense Spoke

Many of the key leaders in the young nation were highly intelligent, extremely well-read, and very curious.

They studied history and governments, recent and ancient.

They studied relatively recent or emerging political and economic theories, such as those of John Locke and Adam Smith.

They corresponded, talked, and debated endlessly with one another.

They recognized from many years of personal political experience that governance was an art, but an art that requires a very strong, power-confining foundation.

And they understood that no definition would be perfect, but that they had a grand opportunity to create something that had never been created before.

The Breakthrough

The Framers of the Constitution were not of one mind or harboring the same motivations, by any means. But they did tend to agree on certain things.

To begin with, the Constitution's Framers believed they must limit the Federal Government. Yet, at the same time, the Framers also believed they must have a strong enough government to defend the sovereignty of America and the freedoms of Americans.

Also, the Framers knew, from personal experience with King George and some of their overbearing state leaders in the 1780s, that the reasoning and the hearts of leaders were not in themselves sufficient to guide a country. Rather, a defined Constitution, actually written down, was essential.

And, the Framers believed that peoples' rights are not given by men or governments, but by God, or by Nature, or by Providence—by an Unalterable that stood apart from man.

So, the Framers of the Constitution decided on just who "Caesar" is in America. Caesar is the people bound by a covenant of their own making, capturing these key understandings.

In America, Caesar is "the people, bound by the Constitution."

Not just "the people." No, Caesar is the people, bound by the Constitution.

The Constitution: a document that protected the rights of individuals (e.g., freedom of speech, freedom of religion) from unnecessary and overbearing government.

The Constitution: a document that delegated crucial *but limited* responsibilities to the Federal Government.

The Constitution: a document that astutely incorporated the existing political structures of the individual states for the ongoing governance of the people.

In America, Caesar is *not* a king. In America, Caesar is *not* the often-cited, default answer of "the Federal Government." In America, Caesar *is* the people, bound by the Constitution.

This approach was astounding, elegant, and workable. And it proved to be enduring and successful, when adhered to.

The people, bound by the Constitution. The breakthrough.

THE GENIUS OF PROPERLY STRUCTURING CAESAR

"Freedom Nationally, Virtue Locally"

> "Is virtue a thing remote? I wish to be virtuous, and lo! virtue is at hand."
> Confucius[12]

In the United States of America, Caesar is the people, bound by the Constitution.

But there's really important background to that; this conclusion and the resulting structuring of Caesar has a history.

Americans Rooted in the Long Evolution of English Freedom

Much as many Americans wanted to be rid of King George and England, their perspective of freedom and rights were essentially grounded in the history of individual rights in England.

Ignited by King John's concession to English nobles and agreement to the Magna Carta ("Great Charter") in 1215, England forged an

49

increasing progression of individual rights over the next five centuries. Many of these centuries-long developments in England were foundational to Americans' understanding of the law and individual rights at the time of the American Revolution.

The Profound Inversion of Who Caesar Is

What the Americans did was profound.

The history of England from the Magna Carta to the time of the American Revolution was about English subjects gradually extracting more and more rights from the King of England, England's "Caesar."

In contrast, the Constitution and Bill of Rights specifically enumerated what the Federal Government is empowered to do, and what individual rights are specifically protected (e.g., freedom of religion, freedom of speech), with the remainder reserved to the states and to the people.

Legend has it that the English band played "The World Turned Upside Down" when Lord Cornwallis surrendered to George Washington and the Continental Army at Yorktown in 1781. Little did they know that the song would be far more suitable when the U.S. Constitution was ratified, marking the beginning of "the people, bound by the Constitution" being Caesar. After all, many wars had been won and lost in the long march of history, but a government of self-governing people—now *that* was a world turned upside-down!

The long history of just who Caesar is was profoundly inverted in America in 1791.

The Crucial Distinction:
"Crimes against Persons and Property" and "Virtues"

By and large, Americans naturally carried forward English laws against breach of contract, fraud, theft, murder, rape, and so forth. These traditional "crimes against persons and property" were real crimes that were well-established in the law. The legitimate business of government was indeed to address all such crimes, and remains so.

To be sure, the scope of government is and should be to address real crimes, and the expectation of the Framers was exactly that. And the Constitution does not dispute the purview of the government to address these crimes, but rather addresses the government's proper handling of such crimes in the Bill of Rights, with the individual rights preserved against government abuses (e.g., the right to a speedy trial).

However, what much of the Bill of Rights was all about was protecting Americans from their own government expanding its power beyond handling traditional crimes into the area of personal beliefs or virtues.

Structuring for the
Crucial Distinction at the Federal Level

The Bill of Rights certainly worked to substantially address movement by the Federal Government into private virtues, notably with these two amendments to the Constitution.

★ The 9th Amendment to the Constitution: "The enumeration in the Constitution, of certain rights, shall not be construed to deny or disparage others retained by the people."[13]

★ The 10th Amendment to the Constitution: "The powers not delegated to the United States by the Constitution, nor prohibited by it to the States, are reserved to the States respectively, or to the people."[14]

But, to put even a finer point on it, the 1st Amendment secured citizens' rights to freedom of religion, freedom of the press, freedom of speech, and freedom of assembly.

★ The 1st Amendment to the Constitution: "Congress shall make no law respecting an establishment of religion, or prohibiting the free exercise thereof; or abridging the freedom of speech, or of the press; or the right of the people peaceably to assemble, and to petition the government for a redress of grievances."[15]

This meant that individuals and their houses of worship were free to exercise their full discretion as to their beliefs, virtues, and actions, without undue interference from the government. However, the Federal Government could indeed interfere if such activities were truly treasonous.

So, these Amendments reserved everything that was not delegated to the Federal Government to the States and to the people, and some such reserved rights were very specific to individuals themselves. And, most importantly, the Federal Government was *not* delegated the defining and enforcing of Americans' virtues.

There we have it. *Virtue locally, not Federally.* Truly, traditional crimes against persons and property (i.e., keeping citizens free from criminality, via classic justice) were in the proper purview of government, but virtues were individual or local matters.

This structure can be summed up in four words: freedom nationally, virtue locally.

Freedom nationally, virtue locally.

This was a truly groundbreaking structure for governing a nation. It would be hard to preserve, but it would be worth every effort.

Freedom nationally, virtue locally.

CHAPTER 6

THE HIGH PURPOSE OF FEDERAL GOVERNMENT

Freedom From and Freedom To

"What to the American slave is your Fourth of July?"
From a speech by Frederick Douglass, Abolitionist and
former slave, in Rochester, New York on July 5, 1852[16]

As federal governments go, the U.S. Federal Government has generally been a good institution, when its role is properly executed. That's because proper government is the protector of Americans' freedoms. Which freedoms are key?

★ Freedom for Americans *from* foreign powers, a formidable and exceedingly important task in any era

★ Freedom for Americans *from* criminals, via a number of well-established, proven laws designed to prohibit and punish criminal activity in the marketplace and the personal realm, i.e., addressing those who would rape, murder, steal, defraud others, breach contracts, and so forth

★ Freedom for Americans *from* inappropriate or abusive government itself, such as an individual's right to a trial by jury, right to petition against unlawful imprisonment, and right to free speech

★ Freedom for Americans _to_ live life as they choose, without the Federal Government coercing what religious virtues or secular virtues Americans are to live by—in other words, government that doesn't cram-down national "virtues" to individuals and local communities

That's exactly what the Constitution and Bill of Rights created for the United States: well-defined and well-anchored freedom.

While the Constitution anchored America for freedom via limited government and the Bill of Rights, it also struck at the heart of the slave trade, allowing Congress to later act to outlaw the slave trade, in 1808. And many leaders in America expected slavery itself to die out in a couple of decades. Unfortunately, it took a much greater upheaval to accomplish that.

Freedom and Equal Treatment Under the Law Justly Extended to All

Even though slave-ownership itself was not addressed, the Constitution stood ready—first, resolute in what it already established for anchored freedom and, second, ready for that freedom to be properly extended to all.

And, over time, although painfully slow much of the way, freedom was properly extended to the unenfranchised.

Here are some key highlights:

★ 1860s: The Civil War Amendments to the Constitution (the 13th, the 14th, and the 15th Amendments) addressed the deeply evil practice of slavery. These Amendments abolished slavery, secured rights for former slaves, and secured the right to vote for African-Americans.

This was the defining win for freedom, equality under the law, and the fundamental justice that inherently accompanies true freedom ("freedom-based justice").

★ 1879: Chief Standing Bear won a major Federal court decision after being denied the opportunity to bury his son's body in his Ponca tribe's traditional grounds.

The Federal Government displayed its usual calloused and inglorious approach with its continued breaking of promises made to Native Americans. In this case, peaceful Ponca men, women, and children had been forcibly moved from the modern Nebraska-South Dakota border to modern Oklahoma's Indian Territory. Chief Standing Bear argued that Native Americans should have legal standing under U.S. law and have the right of petition against unlawful imprisonment.

Here is Chief Standing Bear's poignant summation speech to Federal Judge Elmer Dundy:

> That hand is not the color of yours, but if I pierce it, I shall feel pain. The blood that will flow will be of the same color as yours. God made me, and I am a man. I never committed any crime. If I had, I would not stand here to make a defense. I would suffer the punishment and make no complaint . . .

I seem to be standing on a high bank of a great river, with my wife and little girl at my side. I cannot cross the river, and impassable cliffs arise behind me. I hear the noise of great waters; I look, and see a flood coming. The waters rise to our feet, and then to our knees. My little girl stretches her hands toward me and says, "Save me." I stand where no member of my race ever stood before. There is no tradition to guide me. The chiefs who preceded me knew nothing of the circumstances that surround me. I hear only my little girl say, "Save me." In despair I look toward the cliffs behind me, and I seem to see a dim trail that may lead to a way of life. But no Indian ever passed over that trail. It looks to be impassable. I make the attempt.

I take my child by the hand, and my wife follows after me. Our hands and our feet are torn by the sharp rocks, and our trail is marked by our blood. At last I see a rift in the rocks. A little way beyond there are green prairies. The swift-running water, the Niobrara, pours down between the green hills. There are the graves of my fathers. There again we will pitch our teepee and build our fires. I see the light of the world and of liberty just ahead. . .

But in the center of the path there stands a man. Behind him I see soldiers in number like the leaves of the trees. If that man gives me the permission, I may pass on to life and liberty. If he refuses, I must go back and sink beneath the flood.

. . . You [Judge Dundy, representing the Federal Government] are that man.[17]

Judge Dundy justly found for Chief Standing Bear. No more eloquent speech was ever made:

- for freedom and the attendant justice;

- for intergenerational impact of individual rights and the powerlessness of a single individual at the mercy of a powerful federal government, a government focused on virtue-politics of the moment and not freedom of the individual; and

- for a man's stated willingness to be punished if a real crime had been committed, but his unwillingness to be punished by false virtue-politics.

Ponca City, Oklahoma is home to a larger-than-life statue of Chief Standing Bear.

★ 1920: The 19th Amendment to the Constitution granted women the right to vote: "The right of citizens of the United States to vote shall not be denied or abridged by the United States or by any State on account of sex. Congress shall have power to enforce this article by appropriate legislation."[18]

Decades of efforts for women's suffrage finally bore fruit. Early on, the Mountain West had endorsed women having the full fruits of being citizens. In 1869, Wyoming granted women the right to vote; several other Mountain West states followed. The nation at large joined Wyoming fifty-one years later.

★ 1924: The Indian Citizenship Act of 1924 was the true beginning of the end for structured injustices against Native Americans: "Be it enacted, by the Senate and house of Representatives of the United States of America in Congress assembled, that all non citizen Indians born within the territorial limits of the United States be, and they are hereby, declared to be citizens of the United States: Provided That the granting of such citizenship shall not in any manner impair or otherwise affect the right of any Indian to tribal or other property."[19]

★ 1954: The Supreme Court decided the case of *Brown v. Board of Education.*

The unjust debacle of the Supreme Court decision of *Plessy v. Ferguson* in 1896 denied African-Americans free and full access to public schools. Parents in Topeka, Kansas challenged that, and won; the doctrine of "separate but equal" would no longer stand. Freedom and the equal access inherent to freedom prevailed.

★ 1964: The Civil Rights Act of 1964 was enacted: "An act to enforce the constitutional right to vote, to confer jurisdiction upon the district courts of the United States of America to provide relief against discrimination in public accommodations, to authorize the Attorney General to institute suits to protect constitutional rights in public facilities and public education, to extend the Commission on Civil Rights, to prevent discrimination in federally assisted programs, to establish a

Commission on Equal Employment Opportunity, and for other purposes."[20]

This was the full enforcement of freedoms for all. Equal access to public accommodations is freedom *and* freedom's inherent justice.

Though the road had been too long and consistently painful, Americans—by the Constitution, then Constitutional Amendments, Congressional acts, and court decisions—first created the foundation, and then fulfilled the promise of freedom for every American.

In the end, broad freedom was well-established. That is, broad freedom by any reasonable definition in the context of world history.

That promise of real freedom, shamefully rarely-experienced in the long history of governments, is one of the key reasons why so many around the world seek to come to America: freedom sought after, fought for, and fulfilled, however haltingly.

Defending Freedom, and the Spillover Effects to Other Countries

The Federal Government, while rightly fighting to preserve and sustain the freedom of Americans, just happened to win or stabilize the freedom for hundreds of millions of others, either directly or indirectly. Several examples are worth highlighting.

First, the United States' involvement and deep sacrifice in both World War I and World War II played an indispensable role in the liberation of Europe.

Second, at great economic cost, the U.S. immediately followed up World War II with the Marshall Plan for Europe and the transition in Japan to ensure stability and freedom.

Third, the U.S. led the fight in the Cold War. With the collapse of the Soviet empire, hundreds of millions of people worldwide tasted freedom as the world had never seen in the history of governments. The essential bulwark against the Soviet empire's ambition was the United States.

Freedom from Criminality

From the beginning, America stayed true to the English heritage of the rule of law. At America's founding, traditional laws against breach of contract, fraud, murder, rape, and so forth were well-established. These crimes against persons and property in the various states were routinely enforced for the sake of all, with a result of a relative freedom from criminality.

Freedom from Government
Bearing the Sword Too Heavily

Unlike the general heritage of countries in Continental Europe with a civil law structure where the king historically issued a code of law, the English people had ever-so-slowly-but-surely secured rights, beginning with the Magna Carta in 1215. Americans were anchored and experienced in an English understanding and practice of freedom. The

Amendments to the Constitution in the Bill of Rights were key in further anchoring Americans' rights.

Because of this, by 1791, Americans (in a fifteen-year-old country!) seamlessly carried this foundation over and established the right to a speedy trial, the right to a trial by jury, the right to petition against unlawful imprisonment, and other key rights.

In short, Americans created a structure that worked to ensure that the Federal Government could not bear the sword too heavily in the pursuit of handling crimes.

Freedom to Determine Personal Virtues

The high purpose of the Federal Government is to ensure freedom, including those circumstances when individuals seek to thwart or limit others' freedom (e.g., rape, murder, lack of suffrage, Jim Crow-like discrimination in public facilities).

Indeed, freedom for Americans is the high purpose of the Federal Government in America.

Beyond that, Americans retain the right to determine their own virtues, opinions, beliefs, and actions. It is *not* the purview of the Federal Government to define and enforce the virtues of Americans.

Now, that is true of a Federal Government that might want to coerce all Americans into living by Christian virtues. That is, when the Federal Government is a de facto *Christian* theocracy.

And, that is true of a Federal Government that might want to coerce all Americans into living by Secular virtues.

That is, when the Federal Government is a de facto *Secular* theocracy.

However, there still seems to be no shortage of people in power at the Federal level of government who want to cram down their version of virtues for the nation . . .

CHAPTER 7

BEYOND THE BULLY PULPIT

The Apparently Irresistible
Temptation of the Governing
Elite to Cram-Down Virtues

"the right thing to do"
Barack Obama,
when Googling "the right thing to do Obama" on August 26, 2010
to find reports by traditional news outlets and White House press
releases about the Federal Government's justification for action on
numerous issues, for example: requiring all Americans to purchase
health insurance, "age-appropriate" sex-education in public
schools, taxpayer-funded stimulus packages for one of the world's
largest corporations, and Federal "investing" in specific cities

The eradication of slavery in the U.S. was a triumph
of freedom. Abolitionists had worked for decades to
eliminate slavery, but it took the Civil War to bring
the issue to resolution. Freedom won the day.

Virtue-Politics Infects the United States

Just after the Civil War, the virtue instinct of a
number of Americans was codified into national
law, spurred by the efforts of Anthony Comstock.

In 1873, the "Comstock Act" (officially "An Act for the Suppression of Trade in, and Circulation of, obscene Literature and Articles for immoral Use"[21]) targeted "obscene, lewd, or lascivious" items sent through the U.S. mail, including information about contraceptive devices and abortion.

A number of states had also installed various laws addressing such issues before the Comstock Act, but this was the first national law of its kind. The Comstock Act was an amendment to the Post Office Act, and Comstock personally got involved in enforcement as a special postal inspector and was personally vested with the power to arrest and detain.

In policing the distribution of porn, the Federal Government was now officially in the "virtue business." This was beyond the realm of crimes against persons and property. The Comstock Act inherently called for definitions of obscenity, with predictable results: no one could define obscenity to everyone else's satisfaction.

Whatever the good intentions of the Comstock Act in promoting social good, the never-ending battle over virtue-politics and virtue-policy was now prominently engaged at the Federal level. The Federal Government had a real taste of power in the virtue realm, and life in America would never be the same.

Beyond the Comstock Act, many Americans remained very concerned about virtue. Specifically, they had seen the ravages of alcohol abuse on personal lives and on families, and drunkenness offended their virtue sensibilities.

Therefore, temperance organizations thrived, and Americans followed the Prohibition example of a number of

European countries. The momentum to coerce virtue in individuals and families increased, and Americans ultimately took a breathtaking direction. Effective in 1920, to keep ordinary Americans from consuming alcohol—drinking a draught of beer after work at a local pub—Americans outlawed the manufacture, sale, or transportation of alcohol in America. They did this in the form of the 18th Amendment to the Constitution.

The 18th Amendment created at least three consequences. It vastly increased the power of the Federal Government to "police" virtue. It struck a blow to common-sense freedom. And it quite predictably created additional dimensions of criminality to the American culture.

And, was virtue improved?

The American people came to their senses and completely repealed the 18th Amendment with the 21st Amendment in 1933. The issue of alcohol consumption by adults was ultimately relegated to a more common-sense approach. Moderate consumption was once again a private matter, and abusive consumption spilling over into others' lives (e.g., killing an innocent person while driving intoxicated) was properly a crime against a person or property.

Virtue-Politics Goes "Big-Time"

The Great Depression and its deep financial turmoil opened the door for President Franklin Roosevelt's "New Deal" expansion of the Federal Government. The turbulent 1960s paved the way for President Lyndon Johnson's "Great Society." Freedom and local virtues were no longer enough, supposedly—Americans *needed* a so-called Great Society as conceived, designed, and imposed by the Federal Government.

Great urgency was required, of course, with official Federal Government language coined to accentuate the urgency. No longer could we have bland, bureaucratic language. It was now "war." So, it was the "War on Poverty" and, later, the "War on Drugs."

And, while the landmark Civil Rights Act of 1964 was entirely justified and proper in its focus to provide freedom-based justice to African-Americans and remedy true structural discrimination in fulfillment of the promise of the 14th Amendment (Dr. Martin Luther King, Jr., the great champion of freedom-based justice: "Free at last! Free at last! Thank God Almighty, we are free at last!"), it also unfortunately prompted follow-on Federal virtue-politics activity.

By this time, the train had definitely left the station— that is, the Federal-Government-as-decider-and-enforcer-of-virtue train.

America apparently is now experiencing a third great wave of Federal Government expansion in the last eighty years: first, the New Deal of the 1930s; next, the Great Society of the 1960s; and, now, early in the 21st century, it's apparently about the Federal Government "achieving" a Totally Virtuous America.

So, now, in the early part of the 21st century, a "more virtuous" populace *will* buy compulsory health care coverage. They *will*, of course, buy the "correct" light bulbs. They *will* forego fuller employment of Americans to ensure that the delta smelt fish thrives. And they *will* eat less sugar and salt in every product, because the government surely *will* soon require the food producers to look after the welfare of Americans, under—what else?—the Federal Government's guidelines.

And, as we know from the 1780s, and from all of human history for that matter, the people in charge, elected or not, want to force others to the "correct" behavior. Of course, this strongly coercive impulse was in King George. And it was, and is, in every top-down Federal Government.

A Nation of Virtue-Coercers?

Will Americans' virtues ultimately be in the hands of the legitimate American Caesar, "the people, bound by the Constitution"?

Or is Caesar, now, just "the Federal Government"? In other words, will a large number of American people continue to agree with the trend that the Federal Government can impose its virtuous notions on the entire citizenry?

To be sure, almost everybody wants a virtuous country. Many people of 1600s Massachusetts did, and they had a vision that was not compatible with the vision of Roger Williams, the founder of Providence, Rhode Island. Williams founded Providence because of his differences as a serious Christian with Massachusetts, including his belief that Christians should not be forced, by power of civil authorities, to attend church with unbelieving citizens.

The question is, of course, whose virtue?

"Virtue locally" is the prudently best answer, of course. It has been the best answer for over three hundred years in America. The people in Berkeley and Boulder, Dallas and Des Moines, Lancaster County and Las Vegas have established local community values, as the U.S. Constitution allows. The virtues of each local populace—however lacking or laudable to others—have historically prevailed.

Yet, if an American wants to move to any particular locale and use legitimate freedoms of religion, speech, and press to actually persuade others to change their ways and take a different path—well then, power to them. Yes, power to them, whether they be atheist or Christian, vegetarian or full-buffet, pacifist or hawk, environmentalist or materialist, or whatever persuasion.

But those methods of persuasion are not the only things that are happening. Local persuasion is apparently not enough; many cannot resist the opportunity to go further. Whether motivated to secure political office, change the world, save a soul, or save the planet, they want to cram down their virtues or values by the rule of Federal law or regulation.

So, is America becoming a nation of virtue-coercers? Or, is America just electing virtue-coercers to Federal office and letting them run wild?

About a hundred years ago, President Theodore Roosevelt called the U.S. Presidency a bully pulpit. By that, he meant that the office of President was a unique opportunity to persuade others of the best course to follow.

But a number of his successors as U.S. President, from Woodrow Wilson, to Franklin Roosevelt, to Lyndon Johnson, to Barack Obama, have used the Presidency as a "bullying power-grab." In that approach, the U.S. President teams up in varying degrees with a powerful Congress and an unaccountable bureaucracy to define and enforce newly-discovered "virtues" for ordinary Americans.

Just how much courage does it take to monopolistically, often unilaterally, coerce others to "do the right thing" by using the powers of Federal offices? Will the long view of history truly applaud the long list of coercers driving government policies?

When the Federal Government accommodates so many virtue-coercers, freedom—for everyone—is the loser.

Really? A nation of virtue-coercers? That's *greatness*?

CHAPTER 8

IN THE NAME OF VIRTUE
The Federal Government's Institutionalization of Covetousness and Greed

> "You shall not covet your neighbor's house; you shall not covet your neighbor's wife or his male servant or his female servant or his ox or his donkey or anything that belongs to your neighbor." (Exodus 20:17, New American Standard Bible)
> The Tenth Commandment given to Moses and the Israelites by God

Politicians often make a great show of asserting that capitalism—free markets, that is—practically invented greed. And by greed, they typically mean the personal accumulation of wealth.

What these politicians _don't_ mean is the greed of their supporters to get something for nothing _from somebody else_ in the form of unearned entitlements.

And, these politicians _don't_ mean the greed of their supporters who get Federally-funded local infrastructure _paid for by taxpayers elsewhere_.

And, these politicians _don't_ mean the greed of their supporters who are offloading the taxpaying-burden of virtue-projects (such as welfare and universal health coverage) *from "me" to "my neighbor."*

The simple truth is that covetousness and greed are inseparable from the nature of people.

Who Institutionalizes Greed—Free-Market Participants or the Government?

So, is a nation that wants to minimize greed generally best served by free markets, where competing businesspeople convince independent consumers—some greedy and some not, but all self-funding in their decisions—to voluntarily enter into transactions using their hard-earned money?

Or, is a nation that wants to minimize greed generally best served by a coercive, powerful set of legislators who serve a specific group of greedy and covetous constituents? These constituents, whether official lobbyists or merely special interest groups, join together to effectively place representatives in office who would monopolistically take the resources of their neighbors, quite often not for the common good, but for these special interests.

You know, special interests that have received *billions and billions and billions* of taxpayer dollars. The unending list of special interests includes companies such as General Motors and Goldman Sachs, people in favored House and Senate Districts enjoying very expensive Federal boondoggles, and numerous self-identified and widely-heralded "victims" in American society.

So much for common-good virtue. Instead, the greed of some Americans is rewarded, over and over again, while American taxpayers are left holding the bag.

The plain truth is that *free markets are a natural check on the success of greed, while the Federal Government actually promotes and institutionalizes greed.*

Here's why.

If private companies operating in free markets become too greedy, raise prices, and don't serve well, then their customers simply secure services or products from their competitors.

In contrast, if the Federal Government becomes greedy and raises its prices (e.g., taxes and fees) or reduces services (e.g., diminished "universal" health care availability or its delivery-timeliness), then there is no check on its power to stop its monopolistic desires. And that works very well, as long as the wily politicians are careful to feed the covetousness and greed of just enough of the people being favored in the political process. That includes each other, so they agree to all their peer politicians' earmarks and pet projects in exchange for funding theirs.

The first rule of greed-politics is to be very careful to continuously feed key constituents with government largesse and favoritism. The Federal Government does this routinely, all in the name of virtue.

A participant in free markets cannot institutionalize covetousness and greed, but the Federal Government can, and routinely does.

Condemning Free Markets as "Immoral" While Enjoying Their Fruits

A number of people indignantly criticize free markets as inherently immoral and heartless. Some even deliberately avoid rigorous pursuit of robust economic success in the marketplace. Instead, they take only "moderate-paying" jobs, or very secure public-sector jobs. But the irony is that these jobs' desirability depends entirely on the success of free markets. Because of free markets, these jobs' pay scales are at a very high percentile when compared to much of the rest of the world.

So, here's the "moral" position they embrace: these people apparently think they secure a certain moral purity or level of personal virtue by criticizing the "immoral" free markets, even while they themselves thrive because of the prosperity created by robust free markets.

However, these people detesting free markets and capitalism are not moving to Cuba to earn far less on average in order to remain true to their ideology. No, it's always more materially comfortable and savvy to work for "social justice" within one of the wealthiest countries in history. Besides, it's not healthy for residents to criticize Cuban leader Fidel Castro for any lack of Cuban social justice.

Then, these same people typically assert that those who thrive greatly in free markets are somehow "un-virtuous" for excelling at serving ordinary people extremely well every day. Apparently, it's "virtuous" to force people to be "virtuous" by government decree; however, it's "un-virtuous" to participate in purely voluntary, competitive transactions where all parties to the transaction believe they are better off.

Sam Walton and Boris Yeltsin

For example, to these critics, the late Sam Walton, founder of WalMart, is apparently the very picture of wickedness.

Never mind the fact that, for decades, millions upon millions of people are clearly better off, because Walton served them, employed them, or purchased from them. These Americans freely transact with WalMart in various ways, and thus "vote" on a routine basis for a better life. For example, by their voluntary participation in the marketplace, consumers believe they acquire the necessities of life for less cost from WalMart. In this way, they free up their resources to help others less fortunate, or to use freely elsewhere, however they are inclined.

But many who criticize entrepreneurs such as Walton, some of whom would make a show out of never patronizing Walton's stores, *still* benefit from the marketplace's lower prices and better delivery that were spawned by Walton. That's because they shop at WalMart's competitors who were compelled by the WalMart-driven marketplace to quickly deliver products for lower prices.

Here's an interesting contrast to the likes of Sam Walton. Boris Yeltsin was a member of the Communist government elite in the USSR (Union of Soviet Socialist Republics). Yeltsin was famously stunned in 1989, when he visited a Houston, Texas supermarket and observed the shoppers' immediate access to a huge variety and selection of food that Americans routinely enjoy. That was a dramatic contrast to the Soviet people who routinely waited hours for a very limited selection of goods. Yeltsin reportedly spent his next plane flight from Texas to Florida bemoaning what the Soviet Socialist system had done to its people.

Fortunately for Americans today, President Lyndon Johnson and his compliant U.S. Congress did not create a comprehensive program in the 1960s for "universal food care," defined and enforced by the Federal Government, as part of his overbearing, "virtuous" Great Society push. If the Federal Government had done so, Americans surely would now experience far higher food prices and far fewer choices in their diets. And, in 1989, Boris Yeltsin likely would not have been astonished at all.

"Virtuous" Federal Government Takes Action

So, these critics detest free markets and the people who succeed while participating in them. Therefore, it follows that it is virtuous for the Federal Government to take a much higher percentage of resources from these more-successful-in-the-free-market-than-I-and-therefore-unvirtuous people (such as Sam Walton) and then give those resources to themselves and their constituents in the form of Federal Government salaries, Federal Government services, special Federal projects, or Federal entitlements.

Aha! The critics have played the virtue card once again. They not only rhetorically place enthusiastic participants in free markets such as Walton on a supposedly lower moral plane, they also "help people" by ensuring that

Federal Government power plays a vital role in transferring the "greedy" entrepreneurs' wealth to others.

But the unfortunate reality is that covetousness and greed are fostered in the recipients of government largesse. And, over time, that covetousness and greed are institutionalized into a rock-solid entitlement mentality.

Of course, the customary rhetoric is that the Federal Government is taking these actions for "the least of these." That's the Bible phrase used by politicians and bureaucrats to mean transferring Peter's wealth to Paul, with every transfer including hefty handling charges (i.e., government salaries and political IOUs). After all, the politicians and bureaucrats must be very well-paid for managing the bureaucratic transactions of collecting taxes and spending those collections.

A straw-man argument? Hardly. This type of thinking is routinely assumed and peddled in many universities and by many media outlets, not to mention a number of reliably sanctimonious politicians.

Using the anti-free markets rhetoric and playing the "victim" card, the Federal Government demagogue transforms covetousness and greed into "virtue" and "social justice." The Federal Government's exclusive control over citizens forces reallocation of resources to special-interest-favored sectors of society.

Whose Stewardship is Better?

All this government intrusion, *as if the Federal Government is a good steward of taxes collected.* Intentions are one thing, actual results are another. For example, President Lyndon Johnson's War on Poverty was actually a War on Families, where the government's rules worked to destroy families and actually keep participants wedded to government largesse. President Johnson's "virtuous" policies ended up encouraging the wedding of individuals to the Federal Government, not weddings between a man and a woman.

The very nature of a Federal Government program funding virtues means that *those in Congress passing the virtue legislation do not believe that the American people are better stewards of their own money and better discerners of virtue than the Federal Government is.*

The Federal Government's irreplaceable role is to preserve Americans' freedom. That includes the proper handling of traditional crimes against persons and property (traditional justice) and the ensuring of equal access of all citizens to public accommodations (freedom-based justice). But the Federal Government should not be in the virtue business. Besides, the Federal Government is not competent at defining virtue, and it is not competent at delivering virtue.

The Lobbyist Problem: Powerful Beneficiaries Are Never the Same People as Shunned Taxpayers

Some economists actually study the implications of lobbying in a representative government. Successful lobbying creates, as some economists might say, "concentrated benefits but dispersed burden."

That's a fancy way of saying that a lot of people (taxpayers) share the burden of the funds given to the relative few that get the lion's share of the benefits (special interests). America has seen this system boom for decades, as politicians are substantially funded in their campaigns by simply showing targeted favoritism in legislation.

Then, after their service in Congress, numerous Congressional representatives routinely take very high-paying employment with lobbyist firms. This is a wink-wink way of life that Washington is so desensitized to that it is considered normal, even sophisticated. Yet virtue is expected from these Washingtonians who think nothing of these now-standard arrangements?

But it's becoming worse. What if the politicians can get elected by having 45% of the populace pay for all the whims and desires of the remaining 55%? How easy would it be to get elected and control the U.S. Congress? Pretty easily. And that is exactly where the Federal income tax code has been heading for years, as fewer and fewer Americans pay any income taxes at all.

In other words, the Federal Government inherently institutionalizes greed and covetousness in the 55% at the expense of the remaining 45%. That's the more sophisticated level of the lobbying problem—concentrated benefits and concentrated losses, just different groups!

Killing the Golden Goose

But a nagging problem remains, as told in the old parable of killing the golden goose. Only a gross, or perhaps willful, ignorance of both economics and human nature would allow politicians to believe that this type of approach is sustainable in the long-term. But ideology and short-term political greed often trump common sense and stewardship for *all* the people.

"The least of these" rhetoric and policies that are actually promoting greed and covetousness will kill the golden goose. In this way, the citizens who thought they were getting a free ride from "the rich"—the golden goose—sooner or later end up remorsefully discovering that not enough people are left to support the way of life to which the free-riders had become accustomed.

Theory? Hardly. Once again, Europe is leading with bad ideas and worse policy. In 2010, Greek citizens vigorously protested in the streets because there was little left of the golden goose to tax. And the country is near bankruptcy, begging banana-republic-style debt remedies. Then, there's deep anger in the streets, even *after* outsiders propose bailouts? Anger at whom? The Greek people have no one to blame but themselves, and the government they had asked for, and got.

This is madness, of course. It is nothing but the fruit of greed and covetousness fostered for years by government policy.

The Constitution's Framers Were Ahead of the Problem

The Framers of the Constitution knew all of this. Adam Smith's classic *The Wealth of Nations*, the first popular treatise on free markets, was published in 1776, the same year Americans declared their independence. *The Wealth of Nations* was a smashing literary success for its time. With this and his other writing (i.e., his *The Theory of Moral Sentiments*), Smith painstakingly built the practical and moral case for free markets. And, remember, the Framers had box seats to the overbearing folly of some of the 1780s state governments.

So, there was, *and is*, an answer.

Freedom nationally, virtue locally.

When a community reaches out and supports the needy in their community, that's true American virtue at work! In fact, that actually happens countless times every day in America, via voluntary outreaches and ministries providing food, clothing, medical services, job training, and much more.

And, if a community such as New York City or San Francisco further wants to tax its residents or visitors—sometimes quite heavily—to fund its social priorities, then well done, generous citizens! Over time, the residents who don't like that priority can change either their address or modify their city's policies via future elections.

In all cases, local people—not cloistered Federal employees spending taxpayer money—are best qualified to assess the validity and depth of the needs in their community and can make adjustments in funding and services more easily and quickly.

Freedom nationally, virtue locally.

Is it wise to foster a Federal Government that institutionalizes covetousness and greed among its poorer citizens?

Equal opportunity for every person? Absolutely! Short-term help when once-in-a-generation Hurricane Katrina devastated several states? Most certainly!

But, the Federal institutionalization of covetousness and greed? Why?

Institutionalization of covetousness and greed, in the name of social justice? Is it "justice" to institutionalize covetousness and greed in recipients of Federal Government largesse, putting them in a very real bondage to the Federal Government? Is it courageous? Is it statesmanship?

And all this is done in the name of virtue.

No. There's a better way. There is a way with more direct accountability, personally and politically, for both politicians and their constituents. And that way is to address the needs of the truly poor at the personal level, the community level, or the state level. All these levels of help eventually have to pay their own bills.

Freedom nationally, virtue locally.

CHAPTER 9

WHEN AMERICANS' CHURCH BECOMES THE STATE ITSELF

Well on the Road to a Secular Theocracy

> "All animals are created equal but some animals are more equal than others."
>
> The reigning pigs' final (single) Commandment in George Orwell's *Animal Farm*[22]

A seasoned Jewish man challenged me during the question-and-answer session: "You made a mistake in your speech about freedom nationally and virtue locally. You haven't talked about all the religions-without-God, such as Marxism, Liberalism, Progressivism, and Socialism."

"You are right, sir," I replied. "I didn't bother talking about all those -isms. I simply talked about the 'Church' that those ideologues use to accomplish their particular goals for the whole society to supposedly be much more 'virtuous'—and that 'Church' is the State. By talking about their common thread of the State, I can save lots of time and effort trying to distinguish one from another. If you take away their coercive State, all those types of people are just dusty old college professors."

The audience burst into laughter—they've been around and they've been observant. They know how it really works.

A Theocracy, But Not a Christian One

Put your ear to the political turf and the cable news shows, and you hear that Americans don't want a theocracy. A theocracy: you know, a government ruled by religious authority, with laws and regulations about how citizens must live their lives. Among advocacy groups for various causes, there is no shortage of people worried that Christians want to impose their personal views on everybody else via the Federal Government.

But the vast majority of American Christians don't want a theocracy at all—quite the opposite!

The plain, unvarnished truth is that the vast majority of Christians don't want anything remotely resembling a theocracy. Why do you think there are hundreds of Christian church affiliations (e.g., Baptists, Methodists, Presbyterians, Church of Christ, Church of God in Christ, Assemblies of God, AME, Lutherans)? That's because American Christians can't agree on very much of anything and don't want others' beliefs—Christian or not—crammed down their collective throats.

Indeed, those who call themselves Christians are hardly ever in agreement on any topic, Christian doctrine, or any particular belief about how the faith should operate in the public square. It's been that way since Roger Williams left

Massachusetts to found Providence, since the Quakers con-gregated in Pennsylvania, and, presumably, since two Puritans met in a Puritans-only town-hall meeting.

The problem is, a number of key Americans, at least those with preferred parking in Washington, DC, are *routinely revealing by their rhetoric, and by their actions, that they do want a Secular Theocracy.* You know, a theocracy, a "national community" with religious-like, Federally-enforced laws and regulations that everybody *will* follow to supposed-ly make the entire nation virtuous. But this theocracy is run by a relatively few people *using Secular standards*, without the "God" part that so many simple-minded Americans are clinging to, you know.

Some Key Doctrines of a Secular Theocracy

The modern Secular Theocracy has some doctrines essential for its success. Here are a few definitions *written from a Secular Theocracy perspective*—never actually written down, of course, but well-understood and executed by all the Secular Theocrats.

1. *The doctrine that "the Federal Government is virtue-Caesar, defining and enforcing the nation's virtues."* Top-down power always ultimately resides with a Federal Government. Why go to the hard work of persuading stubborn, ignorant citizens, one-by-one, of the right thing to do for social priorities, when Washingtonians who are the best and the brightest can define brand-new virtues and then actually require everyone to be virtu-

ous? "Federal Government as virtue-Caesar" is by far the most efficient path to a virtuous society, a fair society, a society of equal outcomes. President Lyndon Johnson had it right: a Great Society is courtesy of the Federal Government.

2. *The doctrine of "using deliberately mushy words and terminology."* Straightforward, accountable definitions simply don't work to get the results desired. Terms such as "justice" won't do, because that means a particular person took a particular action that was clearly wrong by objective, clearly defined, and written-down standards.

Instead, phrases such as "social justice" work very well, because nobody can really define social justice. And a definition of "social justice" is not even wanted—because that would limit the vast number of times that the Secular Theocracy can call for social justice and indict the entire society for its neglect of the Secular Theocracy agenda.

However, it is vitally important to use the word "justice" within the full phrase; this works to condemn the people who are not moved to do *something—something really, really important, urgent, and necessary*—as conveniently defined by those in the Secular Theocracy. After all, "justice" demands it.

The trick is to always blur "social justice" with both traditional justice (addressing traditional crimes against persons and property) and freedom-based justice (e.g., equal access to public accommodations) in discussions, debates, speeches, and publications. This works to pre-sume that social justice is of the same importance and on the same, or even higher, moral plane as traditional justice and freedom-based justice.

3. *The doctrine of "never enough."* This is closely related to the doctrine of mushy terminology. No matter how hard the non-believers in Secular Theocracy try to comply with the mushy definitions of needed Secular virtues (as defined by the Federal Government, of course), their efforts are "never enough."

   Here's a sample statement of this doctrine in action: "Once again, Americans' collective attempts at this social justice, or that social justice, are not enough, so more taxes and more Federal programs are coming."

   Here's another sample statement: "Once again, Americans' collective efforts at a green, environmen-tally-laudable lifestyle are not enough, so more rules to improve Americans' behaviors are coming."

4. *The doctrine of "original sin."* Americans are all sinners against the necessary Secular Virtues. No exceptions.

   For example, each American has a "carbon foot-print," so every American is hurting the environment and is a sinner. Therefore, the Federal Government must of course determine the extent of each American's sin, the penalty for that sin, and the ever-shifting standards needed to be "without Secular sin." The ever-shifting standards help fulfill the doctrine of "never enough."

Here's another example. Compulsory health coverage will of course necessitate that the Federal Government police the diets of all Americans. So, the latest Federal-Government-funded-and-approved research will surely constantly change to determine just how much salt and sugar will be allowed by the surely-coming and soon-indispensable "Federal Salt and Sugar Division" of Health and Human Services (HHS). Americans' responsibility will be to keep up with the changes made by Washington bureaucrats, or suffer the consequences.

5. *The doctrine of "indulgences."* This handy tactic is borrowed from the pre-Reformation Christian Church of the late Middle Ages in Western Europe. And it is essential.

Some of those in vital agreement with the Secular Theocracy will be given a pass for their original sin when they don't meet the standards that have been set for "everybody."

Here's one example. The leading environmentalists with huge carbon footprints from multiple personal mansions and private planes will be able to buy "credits" to absolve them of Secular sin.

And special, very targeted provisions in Federal legislation, such as tax breaks for favored specific constituents and supporters, will be routine.

A system of "never enough" must also have indulgences, so that the behavior of the favored elite can be rationalized away, and so that the Secular Theocracy's key supporters can be rewarded by ignoring their Secular sins, even while their peers are held accountable.

6. *The doctrine of "the Federal Government always defines 'Neighbor.' "* The Secular Theocracy must have complete control over the definition and classifications of "Neighbor."

For example, a Mexican citizen illegally in the United States, taking advantage of various U.S. taxpayer-funded social services—well, he's definitely a Neighbor for Secular Theocracy purposes. That's because he's a voting constituent, created merely by his presence on U.S. soil. In contrast, his brother, a Mexican citizen barely scraping by economically in Mexico, minding his own business—not a Neighbor.

Of course, the Secular Theocracy has obstacles. Say a U.S. taxpayer makes plans to spend his personal funds to help the Mexican citizen south of the border. And he does not want to send that very money to Washington to fund the health care of the Mexican citizen living illegally in the United States. Well, that taxpayer is racist. Why? Because the doctrine of mushy terminology rules: "racist" is whatever the Secular Theocracy says it is to suit its purposes of the moment, time and again.

Narrow allocation of broad taxpayer resources is of paramount importance, because that narrow allocation drives voter loyalty. For example, spending taxpayer-funded Federal resources ensuring that surgically-transgendered people enjoy the fullest entitlements of a new-found physicality is *necessarily* more important than a taxpayer instead personally spending those resources in private charity to rescue young women from sex trafficking around the world.

Neighbors: whoever rules, defines. The Secular Theocracy defines Neighbor. Ordinary citizens do not.

7. *The doctrine of "the Federal Government commands how Americans will love their Neighbors."* The Secular Theocracy's social justice demands that Americans love their Neighbors, but that isn't the end of the story: citizens must love their Neighbors exactly however the Federal Government instructs them.

Some of the Federal Government's "instruction" is financial, such as higher taxes on all citizens, with the resulting financial distribution targeted to helping-the-Secular-Theocracy Neighbors.

Some of the Federal Government's "instruction" is behavioral. Just who will Americans associate with, and where? The Secular Theocracy will instruct Americans, and all of the instructions are mandatory. Penalties will be severe.

So, here's an example of how "loving your Neighbor" works. Private organizations who are not Secular-Theocracy-friendly surely will be compelled to embrace the transgendered person ("God made me this way!"), while the billionaire driven to employ thousands of people and earn piles of money ("God made me this way!") will be punished by extracting taxes on the fruits of his compulsive, unappealing behavior. Of course, it doesn't matter how "God" really makes a person, it's up to the Secular Theocracy to determine which is good and which is bad, according to the political needs of the moment.

8. *The doctrine of "results don't matter, only good intentions matter."* Whether before a Federal social-justice program starts, or after it fails, the Federal Government's activities are entirely justified by its good intentions. And the cost to the taxpayers is simply not important.

9. *The doctrine of "non-neutrality."* "Secular" definitely doesn't mean neutral. "Secular" must defeat all competitors for the hearts and minds of a critical mass of key voting constituencies and campaign funders. This control only comes with all of the preceding doctrines being in play. The Secular Theocracy is especially not-neutral towards the Christian faith—unless or until Christians submit to the policies and power of the Secular Theocracy.

10. *The doctrine of "Rules about Rules."* These rules are to be communicated to ordinary citizens. First, The Rules are Made by Someone Other Than You. Second, Specific Enforcement of The Rules is Determined at the Whim of Someone Other Than You. Third, The Specifics of The Rules May Change at Any Time. Fourth, The Rules Themselves May Change at Any Time, Without Notice.

The most brilliant political satire of the 20th century was George Orwell's *Animal Farm*. Some say *Animal Farm* was the definitive satire on socialism. But, more importantly, it is a great example of a Secular Theocracy and several of its doctrines for accomplishing the Secular Theocracy's priorities. The ruling pigs in *Animal Farm* fulfilled this particular doctrine of the Secular Theocracy perfectly.

11. *The doctrine that "only the Federal Government can solve these problems."* Got a business too big to fail? Got huge social justice opportunities? Well, friend, the only answer is the Federal Government!

12. *The doctrine of "no grace or forgiveness."* There is no grace or forgiveness for ordinary Americans breaking the doctrines of the Secular Theocracy. If there were grace and forgiveness, then the don't-know-what's-best-for-themselves citizens could escape the rule of the Secular Theocracy.

Well, it's not the Ten Commandments. But it *is* Twelve Doctrines of the Secular Theocrats.

Doctrines for Americans to live by. Doctrines for *you* to live by. Doctrines for *me* to live by. Doctrines for our kids and grandkids to live by.

Whether we like it or not.

When Americans' Church Becomes the State Itself

It's not surprising that the Secular Theocrats are often the first to want the "separation of Church and State."

That's because *their* Church *is* the State. The State is the vehicle by which Secular Theocrats "improve" society and its virtues in accordance with their supposedly superior belief systems—it's their Church. And this "improvement" is typically largely done at the expense of others.

The State has monopolistic lawmaking power. And life is much easier if the Secular Theocrats' chosen Church—the State—has no competition challenging its morality or its rationale for why and how it is exercising that power, such as competition from the Christian Church.

Now, mind you, few, if any, Secular Theocrats claim they're members of any such thing as a Secular Theocracy. And, believe it or not, many don't think they are Secular Theocrats. However, they do just happen to "know" that the Federal Government absolutely must take action and expand its control whenever there is the next "crisis," another "virtue opportunity," or yet another "virtue problem."

But one doesn't measure the Secular Theocrats' membership based upon formal membership rolls. One measures it by how closely they adhere to the Twelve Doctrines.

However, the Secular Theocracy isn't even remotely a conspiracy theory. The Secular Theocrats dearly love those people who are conspiracy theorists. That way they can publicly marginalize the conspiracy nuts.

No, the Secular Theocracy actually operates completely out in the open and has been doing so for years. And it uses kind, gentle, and silky political language, such as "the least of these," and "social justice," and "the right thing to do"—you know, the mushy definitions.

Who this side of heaven knows about the label of "Christian"—only God knows the hearts of people. But, for all practical purposes, some who call themselves Christians are, to all appearances, effectively Secular Theocrats. These Christians are genuinely happy to submerge or even conform the focus of their small-god church to the national-virtue-defining-and-enforcing "Church of State." After all, the nation's social justice "problems" are conveniently presumed to be too big for the private efforts of the American people and the Christian Church to handle.

Why is the Secular-Theocratic Federal Government fittingly labeled the "national-virtue-defining-and-enforcing Church of State?" Well, because the "Church" role *presumptively defines* "national virtue," while the "State" role *vigorously enforces* "national virtue." And the full power of the State is behind the penalty-laden enforcement of the Church of State's numerous laws and voluminous regulations.

Having your organization, the Church of State, control both the definition and the legal enforcement of virtues is *very* convenient and tidy. That is surely gratifying to every would-be King George in every nook and cranny of the Federal Government.

Pity the poor Churches outside the State that have to rely merely on moral persuasion.

Secular Theocrats come in all ethnicities. Some are country club members, some community volunteers, and some marathon runners. Political party affiliations can mean little, or even be misleading. In other words, the Secular Theocrats come from all walks of life.

They often offer well-worn platitudes, just wanting "a better world, a more just world, for everybody."

They are relieved, even overjoyed, that the Federal Government is taking care of it all. Simply write one check to the Church of State every year, if you pay income taxes. If you don't, well, that's OK, brother, because the Church of State knows you are a hapless, financially-strapped victim of capitalist oppressors, such as the pizza parlor owner with her business located in the strip mall just down the street.

Welcome to the Church of State, where nobody is turned away if their allegiance and vote can be counted upon.

Otherwise, the non-believers in the Church of State can be led away to the glue factory like poor Boxer, the horse of *Animal Farm* fame.

The End Result:
"Virtue-Socialism" and "Economic-Socialism"

Socialism has pretty much historically been considered an economic philosophy or system: a Federal Government controlling the means of production and leveling the economic results for people.

But what the Church of State doggedly pursues is really both economic-socialism *and* virtue-socialism. The two goals are to force the leveling of wealth through the government's redistribution of private resources (economic-socialism) *and* to force the leveling of virtues by government laws and extensive regulation of behavior (virtue-socialism).

Of course, the Secular Theocrat would likely say that the leveling of virtues is a leveling "up," a betterment of virtues, according to their clearly superior beliefs. And so we return to the romanticized notion of the Secular Theocracy that the Federal Government can actually define virtues and then deliver virtues, all for the supposed betterment of an entire nation. This system is being installed every day in America, ever more deeply.

But, of course, the reality is that the Federal Government only *lowers* the standards and vulgarizes the virtues of a people already inclined to pursue traditional virtue. The late U.S. Senator Patrick Moynihan of New York coined a clever phrase that describes when a society starts accepting lower standards and creates new, lower norms: "defining deviancy down."

That's the Federal Government, all right, supposedly installing the highest of virtues for all of America, all in a self-laudatory manner.

Again, remember this: *when Americans ask the Federal Government to deliver both freedom and virtue, they will ultimately get neither.*

In a modern representative government, the only antidote to the Secular Theocracy, the Church of State, and the end result of virtue-socialism and economic-socialism is "freedom nationally, virtue locally."

And it's been there all along.

CHAPTER 10

HOW THE "CHURCH OF STATE" ROUTINELY CO-OPTS AND DEFEATS CHRISTIANS

Christians and Their Ever-Failing "Haman Strategy"

> "Behold, I send you out as sheep in the midst of wolves; therefore be shrewd as serpents, and innocent as doves." (Matt. 10:16, New American Standard Bible)
>
> Jesus

The modern Church of State is where elitist Federal Government employees define, then institutionalize, "virtue" for millions of Americans, and reduce their freedoms in the bargain. In the battle for defining and delivering virtues, the Church of State has made a virtual art form of co-opting certain Christians and defeating other Christians.

Many Christians are Serving the Church of State Agenda, Even When They Think They are Fighting It

Christians can be quite interesting in their beliefs and resulting behavior. Take a look at some evangelicals.

These evangelicals assert that America is a "Christian nation." But they conveniently count a huge portion of Americans who are merely cultural Christians. A cultural Christian is someone similar to your second-cousin, Fred, who limits his Christian devotion each year to buying presents for others at Christmas and attending the annual Easter service just to please Aunt Agatha.

At the same time, some Christian-nation advocates study the ever-emerging research that reveals just how weakly understood and shallowly practiced the Christian faith is in much of America. Because of this evident contradiction between America being truly Christian and the research, these advocates sense that the declaration of a contemporary Christian nation is a real stretch.

The apparent remedy is to prove the current-Christian-nation claim by pointing out the truth that many of America's Founders were Christians, and that the dominant culture in America at the Founding was clearly Christian. But that assertion itself presents a real problem for evangelicals. These same evangelicals say you can't be a Christian just because your grandparents were, because every person has to make a personal decision for Christ, i.e., be born-again. If you can't be a Christian just because your grandparents were, how can America automatically be Christian just because many of the Founders were?

Everybody enjoys an echo chamber among fellow true-believers, and contemporary American Christians are no exception. But if they want to preserve or even replenish a nation full of Christians, they will have to stop reassuring each other that America is a Christian nation and do it the old-fashioned way: make Christian disciples of their neighbors. You know, the way Jesus said to do it, the way Jesus in fact *did* it.

Also, along these same lines, American Christians generally want a "righteous nation." Some Christians want a righteous nation because the Bible says that "righteousness exalts a nation." Other Christians want a righteous nation because that seems to conform to the worthy behavior expected as a result of their faith in Christ.

So how do these Christians often play into the hands of the Church of State?

These two desires, to maintain a Christian nation and to create a righteous nation, have worked to entice a number of Christians to focus on and engage in Federal virtue-politics. These Christians take the bait and self-defeatingly respond to the Church of State whenever it pushes national virtue-politics to the forefront of the public agenda. The Church of State does this, unrelentingly, in order to feed its omnivorous appetite for power, control, and beholden constituents.

This is further complicated in that large numbers of Christians have had enormous impact via boots-on-the-ground ministries and outreaches that truly help a lot of people with real social assistance—food help, family ministries, prison outreaches, and much more. They are in fact virtuous in their deeds, and some therefore expect their nation to somehow be virtuous, too.

But many Christians also act as if the nation can only be made virtuous by crucial help from top-down, Federal laws. This is particularly striking because the Bible teaches that true righteousness comes only from God—that the law, or even following the law, is unable to create righteousness.

Of course, many Christian teachers and leaders have long taught the principle that "the law is a moral guide." That's music to the ears of the Secular Theocrats, because as these Christians teach this principle, the Federal Government is busy passing laws and creating regulations about "correct" light-bulb usage, Federal funding of abortion, and thousands of other Secular-virtue priorities.

Here, such Christians have mixed their own toxic cocktail of "Christian nation" and "the law is a moral guide." They have been lulled into the role of the wrong kind of sheep, embracing wherever their Secular shepherds in the Church of State take them. In fact, the laws and the leaders are often neither moral nor Christian. No, it's rudimentally clear that laws can be either moral or immoral. And it's the same for leaders.

The more that American Christians (or any Americans, for that matter) engage in Federal virtue-politics—top-down—the more they follow the playbook of the Secular Theocrats running the Church of State. The Secular Theocrats actually want the Christians to talk virtue-talk and to set up political virtue-platforms nationally.

Then, the Secular Theocrats simply take over the Federal virtue-delivery platform to serve their own purposes.

In short order, America is rapidly moving to very intrusive Secular "virtues" foisted upon citizens. Soon, the Federal diet-police will surely be called to action in order to ensure health-care costs stay low. They will surely be found saying, "Too much salt on your salad, there, Buford. Call in the Federal Salt and Sugar Division Enforcement Group for appropriate action."

The George W. Bush Administration followed the Secular Theocracy playbook perfectly in its rhetoric about "compassionate conservatism" and in some of its policies. Prime policy examples were its well-meaning No Child Left Behind Federal-nannyism in education, its policy of increasing the percentage of low-income loans mandated in Fannie Mae and Freddie Mac portfolios,[23] and its newly-formed White House Office of Faith-Based and Community Initiatives (now operating under different management, values, and labeling, *of course*).

With such policies, the Bush Administration *inappropriately* affirmed many Americans' expectations that the Federal Government should be in the virtue business. And they did this from a supposedly politically-conservative position. Since those types of policies expand the Federal Government's programs and power, the Secular Theocracy will simply take over and once again increase the Federal Government's power to "improve" the nation's "social justice."

Perhaps the Bush Administration was simply very savvy in the necessary-to-succeed virtue-politics of the time.

But perhaps not.

The "Haman Strategy"

Essentially, the Christians who engage in Federal virtue-politics have adopted a "Haman Strategy," an approach that plays right into the long-term game plan of the Church of State.

Here's the story of Haman. In the Old Testament Book about Esther in the Bible, Haman was the King's right-hand man. Haman hated Jews. Haman built gallows explicitly for the hanging of the innocent Jewish leader Mordecai. But the king, husband of the Jew Esther, ultimately hanged Haman on his own gallows.

So, here's the Haman Strategy. Haman planned how others would conform to his wishes, overestimated his power and its sustainability in the political process, devised his strategy without due regard for the actions and reactions of key political players, and had his very designs for others ultimately used against him.

Haman was evil. And authentic Christians are not evil.

But similar to Haman and his strategy, the Christians pursuing virtue via Federal policies are simply over their heads strategically. They sincerely desire virtue for the nation, use virtue language (instead of simply using freedom language) in their national political discourse, and are happy whenever they win individual battles at the Federal level. But what they don't factor in is that only the Church of State is the ultimate winner when Christians engage in Federal virtue-politics.

The Church of State is actually well-served when Christians win some Federal virtue-politics battles. These battles are often ones that many American Christians would not support at all without a specific or implied Christian label, such as the creation of the White House Office of Faith-Based and Community Initiatives. In this way, the Church of State may be granted more wins as part of the political horse-trading of "Federal virtues" in play. Or, the Church of State may expect to simply convert Christians' supposed wins over to the Church of State's win column later. Sometimes, both tactics may be working simultaneously.

A taste of such supposed success tends to keep these Christians' appetites whetted to think they are being successful overall. The king in power hanged Haman, and the Church of State will hang Christians on their own gallows of Federal virtue-politics. That's because the Secular Theocrats control the actual machinery of the Federal Government.

The Secular Theocrats routinely scrub out any hint of Christian stewardship or influence and recast whatever is delivered into a Secular Theocracy framework that institutionalizes covetousness and deepens the loyalties of already-beholden constituents.

Expansion of the Federal infrastructure—even when it starts with Christian motivation or labeling—virtually always *ultimately* works in the Church of State's favor, constantly increasing its power.

Along those lines, here are a few short questions.

First, over the past eight decades, how much Federal virtue-legislation was justified in the hearts and minds of many as the "Christian" approach, or was motivated by Christian principles? A huge portion, of course.

Now, how much of the execution of that Federal legislation has worked to achieve truly moral results? How often has the Federal Government cunningly distributed benefits directly to current constituents while pushing the staggering burden to pay for those benefits back to later generations? How much Federal legislation has worked to institutionalize covetousness and greed? How much Federal activity has reflected the good stewardship that Christians must pursue? How much of the extensive Federal infrastructure has worked to glorify God? How much of that Federal activity has worked to actually fight and diminish Christianity? Sadly, the answers are all too obvious.

And, of course, the Church of State still keeps funding its priorities in the form of taxes.

It's ironic that some of the people fighting traditional virtues in any level of government forty years ago often said that "you can't legislate morality." The Secular Theocrats of this generation, who are routinely defeating Christians, haven't been saying that recently. That's because now that they firmly hold the levers of Federal power, they are legislating and cramming-down *their* version of morality. You know, such as the latest progressive morals embedded in their sex education curriculum targeting Americans' youngest children in public schools.

Here's a key operating strategy of the Secular Theocrats: let the Christians sell it to the faithful, then let the Christians build it, and then let the Christians continue to philosophically and financially support it long after hostile-to-Christians Secular Theocrats have taken over its key leadership from within.

This type of approach worked within America at higher-education institutions such as Harvard, Yale, and Princeton—founded as distinctly Christian institutions and now thoroughly secular.

It worked in a number of European governments.

And, make no mistake, it's working at the Federal Government level here in America. Every time that Christians agree to increased scope in Federal Government—even if it's apparently a short-term win for them—it's definitely a long-term win for the Church of State.

The last hundred years of evidence is that many leaders in modern representative governments with a substantial Christian national history, from Hitler's National Socialism to the modern democracies, simply co-opt the loyalties of Christians, retain an illusion of Christian influence on policies and process, and ensure that the long-term sustainable victories are secular in nature, not Christian.

Unfortunately, many American Christians remain essentially top-down in their political outlook. It is truly amazing that many Christians still actually think they can co-opt the State with classic Christian Church priorities.

Christians' Haman Strategy simply results in self-inflicted defeat.

Bringing Christians to
Moral Submission to the Church of State

From the Church of State perspective, there are two broad types of Christians: those who actually want to be co-opted by the Church of State, and those the Church of State tries to win over. Over the last few decades, at least two key issues have emerged as effective leverage points over Christians: the environment and social justice.

Those Christians who want to be co-opted into the Church of State's efforts are obviously easy victories. Federal initiatives addressing social justice and green issues feel really good to these Christians, and it's not hard for the Church of State to secure their deep loyalty. Of course, a number of these Christians are very sacrificial in their personal lives, in hopeful alignment with such Federal initiatives. Others of these Christians simply prefer offloading their understanding of societal obligations to "the wealthy."

The second group of Christians is more of a challenge.

Many of these Christians have been committing significant, sacrificial personal resources worldwide to truly needy people for years. Their efforts have been on feeding programs, medical outreaches, well-drilling programs to provide clean water, orphanages, children's education, sex-trafficking-rescues, micro-lending for jump-starting successful entrepreneurial activity, enhanced agricultural practices, and so forth. And, these Christians have also been very effective within the U.S. along the same lines, volunteering routinely, founding many programs, and giving hugely substantial amounts away to private charities.

Their hearts are in the right place, but their time and resources in doing so are not under Federal Government control and direction. Therefore, the Church of State first has to convince these Christians that the needs in America are as acute as the needs elsewhere and are still unmet despite the Christians' efforts. Then, the Church of State must convince them that the Federal Government is the right agency to do it.

Why Certain Christians Strongly Resist the Church of State

Convincing these Christians is a tough job. They know that the deep international poverty of hundreds of millions of people is at a completely different level than the relative poverty of the poor in the United States. While these Christians are helping people internationally who might earn, say, $50 or $80 per month, American recipient-constituents of the Church of State range from economically-disadvantaged individuals, to large American cities, to major corporations reaping huge sums from Federal coffers.

Even when the Church of State is directly focused on individuals, these Christians closely observe the programs and often come to believe that the Church of State simply has no effective, locally-responsible, accountability mechanism to accurately and wisely distinguish between legitimately needy individual Americans and "entitlement artists" simply harvesting cash from the Federal Government.

So, these Christians understand the truly effective route to help the needy in America. First, keep an eagle eye on the real needs to be addressed. Second, keep the outreach private and local. Third, practice very attentive local stewardship. This understanding is rooted in these Christians' active experience, presence, and participation in many local, non-government charities. Virtue locally.

For just a moment, set aside the understanding that the Federal Government should not be in the virtue business.

Before a dime of taxpayer resources is even considered, these Christians conclude that the burden of proof should be on the Church of State as to why their Federal programs and processes are needed, and why they are superior in stewardship and social justice to private charities of all stripes. And they believe that non-Christians—really, all people, including Secular Theocrats—who have a passion for helping the poor should do exactly that, but through the local, accountable charities of their choosing, not through ineffective Federal Government programs.

Consequently, a huge difficulty for the modern Church of State has been long-developing: the relative ease of modern travel and enormous advances in technology and communications have truly shrunk the world dramatically. Far from ignorant about conditions both in the U.S. and internationally, these Christians have a very formidable understanding, a broad understanding, a real-world-experience understanding of *genuine, directly-accountable-to-funders, non-politicized social justice*—one that eclipses that of the Church of State and is getting increasingly difficult for the Church of State to defeat.

Here's the story as it unfolds.

First, these Christians see hundreds of millions of deeply needy people—those with barely drinkable water, true lack of food and medical care, vast education-opportunity deficiencies—outside the U.S. They often observe these people firsthand; at a minimum, they learn about them secondhand from the reliable witness of personal friends.

Then, they give sacrificially to help these people via their churches and non-governmental non-profits, with the funds directly applied to boots-on-the-ground local-in-the-Mexican-or-African-or-Asian-villages outreaches.

These Christians are convinced that the Church should always serve the truly needy—these Christians themselves unreservedly support and have been large funders of many such services. So, they naturally study the historical record of generally free-market economies significantly improving the lives of huge swaths of large populations, as compared to the giving impact of churches and nonprofits. That comparative study is firsthand, as they critically assess the effectiveness of even their own ongoing, voluntary, sacrificial, obedient-to-Christ giving.

For centuries, many believed that the wealth in the world was more or less fixed. So, the assumption was that a wealthy person had simply extracted that wealth from poor people. But over the last couple of hundred years, it has become crystal clear that the nations which fostered generally free market economies created massive *new, additional* wealth. And that wealth was quite widely distributed across many of their citizens.

All boats were lifted by the tides of free markets. Importantly, even the characterization of what poverty really means has been radically changed wherever generally free markets are allowed to truly thrive over a reasonable period of time. So, typically the relative poverty in the prosperous U.S. bears no resemblance to the abject poverty in those countries where markets are far less free or have had less time to develop generally free markets.

Using what they have learned, these Christians understandably become convinced that capitalism and free markets have done exponentially more for the poor than the universal Christian Church's efforts or funding, of which they remain enthusiastic participants.

Meanwhile, they watch the worldwide and U.S. government programs (e.g., United Nations programs, President Lyndon Johnson's War on Poverty). They conclude many of these programs are routinely fundamentally flawed in their delivery, often handsomely lining the pockets of the people either who are in charge or who control the conduit of delivery, especially internationally. They conclude that many of these programs substantially fail in their stated missions, routinely waste resources, and consistently institutionalize covetousness and greed.

They also compare generally free-market economies to the lack of impact, misdirection, inefficiency, and even corruption of Federal and international government programs.

And these Christians understandably become convinced that capitalism and free markets have done exponentially more for the poor than the funding of Federal and international government programs.

Accordingly, they think free markets should be supported and even lauded, not denigrated.

Then they start asking the hard questions. They ask these questions of themselves, and of others.

They ask these questions: Which approach truly succeeds in actually creating a reasonable standard of living, *broadly* experienced by *many*? Does a long-term, foundational nurturing of free markets and property rights, both defined and bounded by a reasonable rule of law, succeed best? Or, does the universal Church's activity in social programs succeed best? Or, do Federal or international government programs succeed best?

They ask this question: Do the typical Federal or international government programs in reality actually work to weaken or even defeat the very free-market infrastructures that historically have helped people the most?

They ask these questions: Even if robust Federal or international government programs may appear to help in the short-term, are such routinely-institutionalized programs even remotely sustainable in the long-term? And, has their institutionalization of covetousness and greed irreparably harmed the local social fabric?

After answering such key questions, *they conclude it is their duty to strongly advocate free markets, coupled with property rights and a reasonable rule of law, as the presumptively first, best, and most sustainable answer to meet the basic needs of the poor and to create a middle-class. And these ordinary people often enjoy affordable products and conveniences easily beyond the imaginations and comprehension of the kings of yesteryear.*

This vision also has other thoughtful dimensions. Here are a few.

First, the dignity of the person made in the image of God is nurtured by being valued by the marketplace for his or her hard work.

Second, the market-generated opportunity in a multifaceted marketplace helps develop every person's unique, God-given gifting.

Third, the marketplace affords opportunities for the common person to serve others honestly, freely, and meaningfully, instead of effectively being subservient to either the State or State-favored cronies.

And fourth, free markets create every-street-corner opportunities for the common person to fulfill previously-unheard-of opportunities for ethical stewardship of resources entrusted to him or her.

Prior to widespread free markets (that is, during the majority of human history), these dimensions were comparatively unavailable.

Also, these Christians often become concerned whether social programs safety-nets put into place by the Federal Government are truly effective as to their stated goals (e.g., the abysmal failure and unintended negative consequences of the extremely expensive War on Poverty by the Federal Government). And they become distressed that such bad programs tend to immediately become so institutionalized.

Last—and this is key—these Christians also know first-hand the extent of freedoms, access to education, reliable infrastructure, and opportunity for individuals to succeed in America. And they believe that, in today's America, every motivated, able person has the platform and opportunity to succeed in America, without depending on Federal largesse.

All of this is powerful: many are convinced that they and their neighbors are far and away better stewards of their money in helping the truly needy than Federal programs are.

Also, their young people often go on both domestic and international outreaches, to actually *do* social justice personally. This next generation compares the rampant, deep, gotta-see-it-to-believe-it poverty outside the U.S. to the relative poverty in America. Then, it can be a hard-sell to convince them that their peers in America should automatically be seen as a higher social priority in the form of Federal Government entitlements than children in other deep-poverty countries in the form of Americans' voluntary giving of time and money.

Secular Theocrats Are in Transparent Denial about the New Era of Wealth Redistribution

The irony of the ongoing wealth redistribution demagoguery by current-era Secular Theocrats is very apparent to these Christians. The Secular Theocrats are simply deliberately ignoring two developments. First, tremendous amounts of new wealth have been created over the past two centuries because of free markets. And, second, the natural, organic distribution of wealth has radically increased—for the significant betterment of the average citizen.

Because of free markets that have exploded over the past two centuries, wealth is routinely created and wealth is redistributed, every day, in literally massive amounts. All parties involved in market transactions participate voluntarily and believe they are better off—wealthier, by their own measure—as compared to other alternatives they researched. And willing workers participating in the transactions are helped significantly. The rise of large, broad, prosperous middle classes has been the result.

And, more than ever, wealth is redistributed every day in significant amounts by charitable giving—voluntarily. And the poor are helped significantly.

But those developments are never enough for the Secular Theocrats, of course. So when the rhetoric heats up, these wealth distribution realities are treated as if they never happened. Why do Secular Theocrats actually act as if the iPod-as-a-common-luxury world of today is the same as the horse-and-buggy era? That happens because the Church of State was left out of the action as the required middleman and therefore missed the opportunity to create ever-more-beholden constituents of the Federal Government.

When multimillionaire professional athletes negotiate their service contracts with the billionaire professional team owners in America, the Church of State will *still* find victims.

The Church of State
Still Presses Its Social-Justice Agenda

After all that recent history of successful free markets and charitable activity, the Church of State *still* weighs in and says (or at least strongly implies) that Americans lack an understanding of social justice; that social justice infrastructure in America is insufficient; that Americans don't care enough about the needy; and that the Federal Government understands these problems in a special way. And, of course, implicitly or explicitly, that more taxes and more permanent Federal infrastructure are both needed.

So, in the social justice arena, the mission of the Church of State is to co-opt every Christian who can be convinced, whether easily or not.

If that doesn't work, then the Church of State works to defeat the remainder of the unconvinced by permanently institutionalizing social justice programs, quickly doing so when they have short-term majorities in Congress.

That's the recent story of requiring of American citizens to purchase health coverage—a massive virtue cram-down, of course, quickly executed by the President and Congress. The political calculation is that the majority of Americans will timidly accept dramatically more government control over their lives. Or, even if some Americans are not timid in their acceptance, the political calculation is that they will not amass enough influence to overturn the new virtue-legislation. Will their political calculations be proven correct?

Christians' Vulnerability to Radical Environmental-Virtues

In the environmental arena, the Church of State has been very successful. A number of Christians have moved *from* the classic Christian understanding of a reasonable steward-ship of the Earth (labeled "creation care" in some Christian circles) *to* the ever-urgent, overbearing, world-wide-coali-tion, full-financial-and-diplomatic-priority of the interna-tional green movement. The term "creation care" can also be easily used for this "virtue" of environment-devotion, no doubt to the delight of the Secular Theocrats who need the mushy terminology to help cram-down their agenda.

Along those lines, the international green movement is morphing its terminology from "global warming" to "climate change," when it suits them. This creates a much mushier guiding phrase for influencing government policy worldwide. This crafty re-phrasing helps move the global-alarm trigger points *from* just global warming *to* atmosphere warming, atmosphere cooling, hurricanes, tsunamis, earthquakes, tornados, droughts, floods, and so forth. These events now can be dutifully reported in just the right context by the Secular-Theocracy-devoted media, with an expert helpfully connecting the local calamity with "climate change."

Such calamities used to be called "acts of God"—termi-nology still often embedded in business contracts and insur-ance policies. However, now that the Secular Theocrats have successfully banished God out of much of public discourse, there's no need to blame Him. Best to ridicule televangelist Pat Robertson for doing that.

No, now such calamities are all conveniently presumed to be man-made, by bad actors. And the federal governments of the world must band together to create more virtuous people, about six billion of them. Of course.

Indoctrinating youth has contributed to this effort immensely. That's the fruit of the public-education campaigns beginning with the first Earth Day about forty years ago. The last few crops of teachers are effectively parroting the ideology that they drank in as students themselves.

Skeptics of all stripes are robustly challenging the radical, pseudo-religious elements of the worldwide green movement. They are attacking it wherever appropriate, both on the basis of its lack of consensus in scientific support and lack of demonstrably-successful solutions. But how successfully?

The Secular Theocracy routinely uses its doctrines, moralizing language, and ever-creeping legislation to manipulate and control huge portions of Americans' personal behavior. To all appearances, that is working well and is well-poised for continued success with regard to environmental issues. And many Christians are allowing, and in some cases even promoting, the mushy terminology of creation care to be a key driving wedge for this Secular Theocratic success.

That's because, in a panting rush to be perceived as relevant leaders, some of these Christians have not bothered to discriminate well, or perhaps even at all, between legitimate stewardship of the environment and the very costly ideology of the government intricately controlling people's lives in the name of environmental virtue.

Leaders, political and religious, who would instruct Americans in this important area of environmental stewardship must be held to a standard of very clearly articulating the practical, important differences between the two visions—the vision of prudent stewardship and the vision of environment-devotion.

And Christian leaders have an additional, special standard. That standard is articulating the *spiritual* differences between the two visions, i.e., not leading Christians into the idolatry of worshipping a false god of environment-devotion.

In this process, every Christian leader runs the spiritual risk of deploying the Haman Strategy. Their well-meaning pulpit-homilies on creation care and environmental stewardship can easily lend crucial credence to—and then be immediately absorbed into—a much more massive Secular Theocracy initiative.

Indeed, in some of the comfortable circles of Christians, creation care appears to be quickly approaching broad acceptance as a major doctrine of apparently vast theological importance. In just one to two short generations, these Christians seem to have substantially moved from highly prioritizing the saving of souls to "saving the planet."

Will large numbers of American Christians soon spend more time devotedly recycling each week ("Jesus as soda-can recycler") than in sharing their faith in Jesus as Savior of souls? How many Christians are already doing so? The Secular Theocrats are surely pleased with the fast-growing submission of targeted Christians to an agenda that the Church of State defines, controls, and enforces.

Christians' Twin Vulnerabilities to the Church of State

The Church of State has found the soft underbelly of American Christianity and will keep plugging away. The Secular Theocrats have identified key issues that have varying degrees of Biblical plausibility and applicability, such as environmental and social issues. Then, no matter the true level of legitimacy, they dress up those pigs to be never-enough-done-for-them dire needs, needs that presumably *only* the Federal Government and the governments of the world can address.

With this strategy, the Church of State in America has been winning practically everything it desires for its *Federal-Government-controlled, always-defined-for-political-advantage, lack-of-true-accountability "social justice"* and for changed individual behaviors in the name of environmentalism. To pretend otherwise is an exercise in self-deception.

Christians and other freedom-cherishing Americans must change their strategy in fighting these and other Caesar-like prerogatives that the Federal Government insists upon in the name of virtue.

"Freedom nationally, virtue locally" is the strategy to deploy against the pretensions and coercive activity of the Church of State.

Fighting "Virtuous" Federal Initiatives and Shedding the Haman Strategy

The pace at which the Federal Government is reducing freedom in the name of virtue and social justice is astonishing.

Americans are extremely generous, by and large. They rightly do not appreciate being slammed (or overwhelmed with new, mandatory, unaffordable Federal virtue-programs) for supposedly being uncaring or ungenerous. By and large, Americans exhibit much charity and justice in their everyday lives. And, when they supposedly fall short, it is not the business of the Federal Government to supposedly be "kinder and gentler" than Americans themselves.

Americans should not take the bait of playing Federal virtue-politics. Christians should not be pursuing Federal virtue initiatives, as their good intentions are absorbed into the Secular Theocracy's programs and processes in order to achieve its own, different ends. So, Christians should shed the suicidal Haman Strategy.

Virtue is a local issue. Freedom is a national issue.

If Americans shed the Haman Strategy, a national freedom coalition can win the day and create the opportunity for freedom nationally and virtue locally.

That restores both freedom and virtue to the rightful owners.

CHAPTER 11

GOVERNING DONE RIGHT

Freedom Top-Down, Virtue
Bottom-Up, and Cascading-Down

> "Reflect how you are to govern a people who think
> they ought to be free, and think they are not."
> English statesman Edmund Burke in 1774, referring to
> England's relations with American colonists[24]

Freedom is the privilege and responsibility of the Federal Government. Top-down.

Virtue is the privilege of individuals, families, churches, and communities. Basically, individuals, plus what English statesman and philosopher Edmund Burke called "little platoons." Bottom-up. Self-governing.

This is reasonable. This is not radical. This preserves freedom. This fosters virtue.

This is governing done right.

"How Does This Federal Legislation Increase or Preserve Freedom?"

This is a reasonable question that should be asked, every time, of any proposed Federal action.

And the freedom to preserve includes freedom-from and freedom-to, with Washington legitimately protecting Americans from criminals and terrorists with appropriate laws and regulations.

Very little of what is done in Washington is freedom-neutral—it either protects freedom or it compromises freedom. But sometimes there are legitimate trade-offs, where Americans give up freedoms to protect their freedom, such as getting scanned at the airport.

Running the Federal Government virtuously as it fulfills its responsibilities is important. But defining and delivering virtue for Americans is not the role of the Federal Government—defining and enforcing virtue should be handled individually and locally.

So, Mr. President and U.S. Congressional Representatives, whether in 2004, 2024, or 2044: "How does every piece of Federal legislation increase or preserve the freedom of Americans?"

Is the Federal Government Rightly Following the Constitution?

It may come as a surprise, but a number of key people in Washington show little evidence of caring about a classic implementation of Constitutional principles. Instead, they care about many other things: getting reelected, and power, and fame, and equal outcomes. And they care deeply about furthering of the Church of State, where there is real opportunity to fulfill the destiny of the Secular Theocracy.

So don't expect to engage in a fruitful debate about the Constitution. To the Secular Theocrat, it's a so-called "living Constitution," which essentially means the Constitution says whatever the Secular Theocrats (or anybody else in power) want it to say. In the living-Constitution philosophy, pretty much *anyone* can say they are following Constitutional principles.

In 2010, Congress passed its monumental health care legislation. Americans were instructed by the new law how to spend a significant chunk of the money in their checking accounts—on health coverage. With regard to this massive virtue cram-down, a sitting member of Congress said, ". . . when the deal goes down, all this talk about rules, we make them up as we go along."

Does it really matter just which elected representative reportedly said this? Sadly, no. Americans have unfortunately grown accustomed, perhaps even perilously resigned, to such philosophies and words from office-holders in Washington. You see, Congress was apparently justified in requiring health coverage of every American, simply because they were seeking to create a Totally Virtuous America.

The issue is not simply about identifying a member of Congress to chastise. Rather, the broader problem is that so many elected representatives disrupt the lives of millions of Americans in the name of virtue. And, they will play the living-Constitution card to do so, when necessary.

So, it's just as well to skip the pretense of a fruitful debate about the Constitution with people who will define what it means any way they wish. That's like bringing a knife to a gun fight.

Rather, the reasonable question that should be asked of and within the Federal Government, over and over again, is this: *"How does this Federal legislation increase or preserve the freedom of Americans?"*

And, besides, that question still fits perfectly into the legitimate, intended, honorable Constitutional framework.

Virtue is Local

Virtue properly resides at the local level, with individuals, in families, and in places of worship—at least in those places of worship where a goal is *not* to kill Americans in the name of religion. You know, religious liberty doesn't include jihad against Americans.

Issues should cascade down to the lowest level possible. Families rule themselves (self-governing!), if there are no crimes against persons happening, such as molestation.

Families bind together into communities of self-government. This gives us liberal communities such as Berkley, California and conservative communities such as Athens, Texas. This is the American genius at work. Let each community rule itself, and stop the virtue-coercion from the national level.

Families bind together in school districts. The local schools should be under local control for real accountability. All this is not rocket science: if the parents and local communities don't care enough to run their local schools right, no amount of Federal standards, involvement, and oversight will work for a child to be properly educated.

However, Federal standards, involvement, and oversight in education *will* work in one sense: the Secular Theocracy—the Church of State—will thrive.

What about State Government?

Actually, a state government has many, but not all, of the same duties as the Federal Government: citizens' freedom-from and freedom-to. As an example, of course, the duty of state government is freedom of its citizenry from criminals. That is, state governments should properly handle crimes against persons and property, but ones that don't fit under a legitimate Federal role for handling crime.

Second is handling true common interests around the state, such as roads and their maintenance, for example.

Then, cascading-down is the right model for state government. Freedom of the state's citizens should be the first mission of state government. Local issues should remain local.

That's why huge chunks of Texas are largely conservative, because many Texas communities are self-governingly conservative.

That's why significant chunks of Massachusetts are largely liberal, because many Massachusetts communities are self-governingly liberal.

And that's why Colorado has a liberal Boulder, a conservative Colorado Springs, and a gambling-town Blackhawk. Local jurisdiction rules—just don't export your values to other cities by the virtue cram-down. Therefore, when the Colorado medical marijuana initiative spills over unwanted, illegal drug-dealing (surprise!) into other cities, the state government should act to preserve the freedom of the affected community's citizens to protect themselves from illegal and harmful drug-dealing.

So, a primary purpose of a state government is to preserve the freedom of local communities to rule themselves, without undue spillover from neighboring communities. That requires common-sense, good-faith representatives to wrangle it out at the state level.

Messy? Sure. But freedom should generally rule for community self-determination, while the state government routinely addresses both improper spillover on behalf of all citizens and crimes against persons and property.

And lastly, no bailouts from the Federal Government. Your state made choices, then your elected officials and your state's citizens live with them.

This is Libertarianism, Right?

"Freedom nationally, virtue locally" is certainly not libertarianism.

Americans rightly don't want strip clubs next to their local elementary schools—that's virtue locally, in action. Pure libertarians typically do not want social conservatism at work in their communities.

And Americans want fully-engaged, real-world foreign policies that protect and preserve freedom in America—

that's freedom nationally, in action. Pure libertarians tend to be isolationist.

Libertarianism has typically fallen short of both freedom nationally and virtue locally.

But credit is due. Amidst the virtue-coercers on the left and the right over the decades, many who call themselves libertarians have been consistently essentially asking, over and over, "Why the virtue-coercion from the Federal Government?"

So, why the virtue-coercion from the Federal Government?

What about Abortion?

Abortion has easily been one of the most divisive issues of the past five decades in America.

The crucial question has always been whether a pre-born baby is a "person." If so, abortion is more readily categorized as a crime against a person.

To many Americans, there is no difference between a one-week-old fetus and a baby ready to be delivered—each is fully a person and each deserves the fullest protection of the law. Many others are not so convinced. Accordingly, for the latter group, there often is a perception of a critical difference between the so-called partial-birth abortion, where a near-term baby is aborted, and an abortion just after a woman becomes pregnant.

So, is abortion a crime against a person, or is abortion merely a virtue issue? Because many vehemently give the crime answer, and because many vehemently give the virtue answer, abortion has been elevated to a dominant issue in American politics.

It is very doubtful that these two viewpoints will be reconciled soon, if ever.

There are two primary outcomes for the next period of time regarding the broad issue of abortion: either the 1973 Supreme Court decision *Roe v. Wade* legalizing abortion stands, or it does not. *If* Roe *stands*, in the eyes of the law the decision to abort is a matter of personal choice (virtue). *If* Roe *is overturned* at the Supreme Court level and the issue is sent back to the states to decide, then each of the fifty states will have to determine their respective positions on abortion.

Let's say 25 states then establish *Roe*-like laws and 25 states broadly outlaw abortion (it is highly unlikely that all fifty states would go one direction or the other). The important practical effect is that those living in a state outlawing abortion and wanting to abort can simply travel to a state or nearby country where abortion is legal.

That leaves the pro-life community with a certain unavoidable reality, whether *Roe v. Wade* stands or is sent back to the states: if pro-lifers really want to truly reduce the abortions performed in America at a time in history when personal time, travel, and expense barriers to getting an abortion are very low, they will have to work to persuade people not to use the procedure. They will need to manage centers for unwed mothers. They will need to promote adoptions. That's a full, three-pronged response, and the late Reverend Jerry Falwell modeled just that.

In other words, they will have to pursue virtue locally—at least as the pro-life community sees virtue—and persuade others to like-thinking.

But shouldn't pro-lifers work for the overturning of *Roe v. Wade* as a matter of conscience? Sure, if their sincere desire is to protect the person that happens to be a pre-born baby. And pro-lifers can work to change the composition of the U.S. Supreme Court in the hope that, ultimately, pre-born babies are actually declared persons deserving equal protection from physical harm under the law.

But, the change that pro-lifers *can truly count on* will happen only via virtue locally. That requires local persuasion and personal influence.

Federal Funding of . . .

Meanwhile, no federal funding of abortions, please. Why should taxpayers fund something that many believe to be a crime against a person? Even if abortion is defined as a right, a la *Roe*, that doesn't mean that American taxpayers should fund it.

Eating popsicles and taking a vacation to Disneyland are rights, too, but taxpayers aren't on the hook for that.

Well, at least not yet.

By the way, are those popsicles sugar-free? The Federal Salt and Sugar Division needs to know.

Other Virtue Issues

No virtues to be introduced and enforced at the Federal level, thanks.

That includes those newly discovered virtues politically positioned in the name of freedom-based justice. In reality, that's the forcing of *new* or *revised* social conventions, coupled with the expectation of de facto special accommodations by an often widely unwilling citizenry. And that's done using the top-down power of the Federal Government.

Rather, freedom-based justice essentially corrects circumstances where the unjustly-unenfranchised are not permitted to fully participate in an *established*, citizen-participation-in-public-citizenship act (e.g., voting, access to public accommodations) solely because of their ethnicity or original-equipment gender.

If you and your friends want your brand of virtue, then convince your real neighbors, the ones you see at the grocery store and in the subway. And no exporting your local virtues to the Federal level as a national virtue cram-down.

So, no new Federal virtue cram-downs. From the left or from the right. Period.

The Christian Church, Culture, and the Church of State

Christianity is not intended to be coercive.

During His earthly ministry, Jesus Christ never coerced a single person into belief or action. He didn't coerce others in the name of social justice, and He didn't coerce others in the name of virtue. Jesus didn't even coerce people to believe in Him.

Jesus did call His followers to personally impact others to the fullest personal extent possible. To make disciples. To serve. To help others. To make virtuous personal choices. To build local, person-to-person communities of high principles, like-mindedness, and like-purpose. Virtue locally. Authentic Christianity. In other words, Yes to bottom-up.

But Jesus did *not* coerce others to be virtuous, to "do the right thing." And, He certainly didn't use the Roman government to coerce others to be virtuous, to "do the right thing." In other words, No to top-down.

Christianity simply will not succeed in making the culture either Christian or righteous because Christians or the Church strongly align top-down with the Federal power structure in a modern representative government. The modern, representative-government Church of State is actually a direct, fierce, cunning, monopolistic, and unrelenting competitor to the Church founded two thousand years ago. *That's why the day that the Christian Church starts relying substantially on the modern, representative-based Federal Government to instill or affirm Christian truths and to create or sustain Christian culture is the day that substantive Christianity starts to decline.*

Any rock-solid progress in making Christianity truly work is accomplished bottom-up and then renewed in local social structures, generation after generation—*that's how both the making of Christian disciples and social conservatism actually succeed.*

A number of Christians across the political spectrum kinda-pretty-much hate to admit it, but they *want* the Federal Government to force their version of the Christian thing on others, whatever "the Christian thing" is for them. Is it compassion, or social justice, or universal health care, or better behavior? Their hope is in the Federal Government to bolster, or leverage, or perhaps even supplant the Church's mission—whatever they perceive that to be, whether liberal or conservative.

And authentic Christianity is the loser. That's because coercive Christianity isn't authentic Christianity at all. And when coercive Christianity is sponsored via the Federal Government in the form of taxpayer-funded social justice programs or religious rules, non-Christians *and even many Christians* can mistakenly start believing that merely good works or following rules for good behavior represent the authentic, full practice of the Christian faith. That is a deeply inadequate rendering of the Good News of Jesus Christ.

What Christians Should Ask of a Federal Government

After the fall of Rome, St. Augustine addressed the issue of mixing the religious and political spheres in his classic *The City of God*, instructing Christians about the City of God and the City of Man. At the time of the Protestant Reformation, hundreds of years later, some of the Reformers articulated their general ideas about proper State-Church structures. Among them, Martin Luther advocated a doctrine of two kingdoms and the "liberty of conscience," where, in the context of the State, a federal government is not to enforce spiritual laws. Of course, no matter the advocacy, Europe and its Christians struggled mightily with these issues and their proper applications.

As various European governments moved to representative governments (e.g., democracies) and those governments matured, supposedly-entrenched Christianity steadily lost its spiritual influence. That was in no small part because Christianity was often integrated top-down with those representative-based federal governments. Like clockwork, the Secular Theocrats first moved in to take over the virtue-platforms established by Christians, and then systematically worked to strangle the influence of the Church. Christians are far better served to never rely on a federal government for "Christian" culture at all.

Federal governments come and go, but the universal Church outlasts them all, and should conduct Church affairs accordingly. That means Christians should ask for only two things to be delivered by a federal government: first, the substantive liberties, including religious liberty, affording the opportunity for the Church and Christians to thrive bottom-up (including creating virtuous families, churches, and communities), and, second, freedom-from and freedom-to. No more, no less.

That's a critical part of the very structure—the Constitution and Bill of Rights—that the Framers, many of them very astute Christians, bequeathed to America.

Abraham Kuyper, the Christian theologian who became Prime Minister of the Netherlands in 1901, stated, "There is not a square inch in the whole domain of our human existence over which Christ, who is sovereign over all, does not cry, 'Mine!' "[25] Perhaps. Political conservatives rightly criticize Communists, Liberals, Socialists, and Progressives for trying to forcefully create a Utopia from the top-down. They are trying to "immanentize the eschaton," as philosopher Eric Voegelin generally framed the issue. But, it is folly, too, for Christians to pursue and expect a top-down Christian Utopia before Christ Himself returns to do it in reality.

That's true whether that pursuit is a *liberal* top-down, political-religious Utopia or a *conservative* top-down, political-religious Utopia, as some Christians can't seem to abandon their ever-failing Haman Strategy to help establish national virtue, top-down. And, again, that strategy simply works to cede control to an ultimately dominant, omnivorous Church of State in modern representative-based governments.

A mere hundred years or so after Kuyper's service as Prime Minister, the Netherlands is famous for red-light districts, drug usage, and secular values. And a well-known politician, Geert Wilders, was recently put on trial for speaking out against radical Islam. The significant neutering of substantive, classic Christianity in the Netherlands and some of its neighbors in Europe has been nothing short of stunning.

Picture a nature documentary we might have seen as children, where one animal painstakingly builds a home, then the next animal predatorily moves into the abode, kicking out the predecessor. The second animal knew the plan all along. Yes, that's the national-virtue-politics Christians getting kicked out by the Secular Theocrats. And it doesn't matter if it has happened before (e.g., in Europe), the first animal still does it again (e.g., in America).

It's simply best to never let *any* group in a modern representative-based government create a national-virtue platform. The Federal Government handles traditional crimes against persons and property? Yes. National virtues? No.

The only way Christians succeed *on a sustained basis* in both continuously influencing culture and individuals for Christ is bottom-up. If that is the way that every square inch is captured for Christ, so be it—Jesus did commission Christians to go forth and make disciples. And bottom-up is the proper framework for *all* citizens to thrive in.

Are Virtuous Leaders Needed in the Federal Government?

So, Americans' virtues are rightly defined bottom-up. But doesn't America still need virtuous leaders in the Federal Government? Well, of course!

America needs Federal leaders who discharge their duties to protect our freedoms effectively, and who do so virtuously.

America needs Federal leaders who really are public servants, serving with the truly virtuous common-good leadership that the Framers of the Constitution so deeply wanted in America's leaders. That means solid laws and appropriate regulations for the truly common-good of *all* Americans.

America needs Federal leaders who will take a virtuous stand and not use the Federal Government to routinely institutionalize greed and covetousness in America.

And, America needs virtuous Federal leaders, with the wisdom and understanding to protect Americans' freedoms and to leave the nation's virtues to individuals, families, and communities.

Taking Action on "Freedom Nationally, Virtue Locally"

If Christians want a broadly Christian-virtuous society in America, they must win it afresh in every generation, bottom-up, in their homes, in their churches, and in their local neighborhoods. They must compete with all the other values and virtues in a pluralistic culture.

Whether they like it or not, they must compete in what's called a religious economy—competing for souls, and the attendant virtue, if you will—to establish authentic Christianity, one person at a time.

In other words, they must do virtue locally.

That assuredly does not mean that Christians should disengage from politics. Quite the contrary!

Christians must become national-freedom activists. And, in order to even do virtue locally (and win the battle one-by-one in a pluralistic culture), *they must actually practice their faith robustly.* That's exercising their religious liberty, the liberty that's protected by the 1st Amendment. And when that religious liberty is under direct and often precedent-setting fire, as it increasingly is nowadays, several organizations are very effectively helping those Christians.

This is not about disparaging the intent of well-meaning people to instill timeless virtues in the nation. It's about which strategy works, and specifically the failure of any currently-seductive, top-down strategy of Christians—a Haman Strategy—to restore the culture.

Alongside Christians, *all freedom-cherishing Americans* must fight the non-neutral Secular Theocracy, they must fight the Church of State—they must fight to establish freedom nationally and virtue locally.

So, here are the actions to take for freedom nationally, virtue locally—to restore freedom and virtue to their rightful owners:

★ work for the success of candidates for *national* office (the President and Congress) who are *first and foremost* committed to fully-engaged freedom-from and freedom-to, as their primary political principle;

★ do not support any Federal virtue cram-downs, even when in agreement with the virtue-direction taken (remember, all virtue-platforms such as the White House Office of Community and Faith-Based Initiatives are ultimately overtaken by the Secular Theocracy, and such programs themselves inherently promote that idea that the Federal Government should be in the virtue business);

★ robustly refute via legitimate political rhetoric that the Federal Government has any role in the virtue-cram-down business, no matter which side of the aisle;

★ work diligently for virtue locally in families, houses of worship, local organizations, and communities;

★ work for the success of candidates for state office who are committed to freedom-first at every level and yet still have the wisdom to prudently arbitrate virtue-issues across and between localities;

★ work to build bridges and a committed, no-nonsense, calmly rational, freedom-focused coalition. That coalition would be across various political persuasions—independents, libertarians, fiscal conservatives, social conservatives, Bill of Rights advocates, moderates, and previously-unengaged people alarmed at the recent coercive actions of the Federal Government. That coalition could include people such as traditionally-politically-liberal Jews who historically have not trusted the perceived virtue-politics on the conservative side. Those Jews now have every reason to distrust the Secular Theocracy revealed, as the Federal Government is more and more ambivalent to radical Islam's designs against Jews and real freedom in general; and

★ work diligently to preserve legitimate religious liberty, fighting the ever-growing Secular Theocracy of our time (the Church of State) by supporting local churches, synagogues, etc. and supporting legal foundations dedicated to real religious liberty and the preservation of the Bill of Rights.

Action is required. Diligent, purposeful, persevering, coordinated, coalition action.

How to Get Both Freedom and Virtue in America

Americans are right to want freedom in America. And Americans are right to want virtue in America.

It's just that any strategies short of "freedom nationally, virtue locally" are, sooner or later, fatally flawed. The Secular Theocrats will simply take over. That's the fruit of their relentless efforts to create a freedom-crippling Totally Virtuous America.

All freedom-focused Americans must pull together in a coalition to defeat top-down "virtues" coerced by those politicians and bureaucrats from the national-virtue-defining-and-enforcing Church of State.

Unless, of course, such Americans truly want to keep hearing from Washington and keep experiencing "the right thing to do," over and over and over again.

CHAPTER 12

THE ONLY CLEAR PATH TO AMERICA'S GREATNESS

"Freedom Nationally, Virtue Locally"

> "It is a rough road that leads to the heights of greatness."
> Seneca, Roman philosopher and statesman[26]

The story of America is truly unique and amazing.

First, the U.S. Constitution created a new Caesar, "the people, bound by the Constitution," astutely balancing the need for a strong national government with individual freedom.

Then, Americans persevered to enfranchise every American, all the way up through the civil rights movement, fulfilling the promise of freedom and equal access to public accommodations for all.

But alongside that, the Federal Government started actively encroaching on individual freedoms. This happened slowly at first, but that encroachment is in high gear and accelerating—Washington is increasingly defining new "virtues" and requiring citizens to live by ever-changing codes of behavior.

So, the potential and promise for America's greatness hit full stride, but the dark clouds had already gathered—many Secular Theocrats had moved into the house of Federal Government, proclaiming both freedom and virtue, but delivering neither.

The Federal Government will never deliver real virtue. And the Federal Government will always struggle to deliver freedom even when it is trying mightily to do so, because "doing freedom" is really hard. Doing freedom is a job for mature leaders, responding to real threats from real people with real power, real weapons, and real maliciousness. The Federal Government needs to focus on its most important responsibility: freedom-from and freedom-to.

The only clear path to America's greatness is "freedom nationally, virtue locally."

Freedom nationally, virtue locally is the only way freedom will be truly preserved, as the Federal Government properly, and virtuously, pursues its high calling: freedom.

Freedom nationally, virtue locally is the only way for virtue to be truly renewed, as the American people properly pursue their high calling: virtue.

And freedom nationally, virtue locally is the only way to defeat the virtue-socialism and economic-socialism being forcibly crammed-down by Washington onto the rest of the country.

Neither freedom nor virtue is guaranteed, even when the right roles are pursued properly by the proper parties.

The Federal Government could well fail at freedom. And the American people may well fail at virtue. But it's worth every effort. One working at freedom, the other working at virtue.

The only clear path to America's greatness—freedom nationally, virtue locally.

CHAPTER 13

THE FINAL WORD
A Careful Yet Bold Rendering

"Render to Caesar the things that are Caesar's, and to God the things that are God's." (Mark 12:17, New American Standard Bible)

Jesus

During His earthly ministry, Jesus Christ never coerced a single person into belief or action.

And during His earthly ministry, *Jesus Christ never allowed others to coerce Him into wrong belief or action. Followers of Jesus—Christians—are called to do no less.*

Jesus instructed Christians to render to Caesar. And the Framers of the U.S. Constitution essentially defined Caesar in America as "the people, bound by the Constitution." And that Constitution quite properly reserved virtues to the people, not to the Federal Government, even while delegating the job of virtuously preserving freedom to the Federal Government.

However, the trend is that the Federal Government inexorably continues to define and enforce Federal "virtues," and, in doing so, the Federal Government is crushing freedom for ordinary Americans.

But, since the Constitution's Bill of Rights reserves virtues to the people, *rendering to Caesar Constitutionally* means handling virtues locally, through individuals, families, houses of worship, and local communities—even when citizens disagree with the virtues that other Americans select.

And, since the Constitution's Bill of Rights reserves virtues to the people, *rendering to Caesar Christianly* means the Christian is personally accountable to God for virtues and proper stewardship in those very same local vehicles.

All the while, the Christian must vigilantly understand the differences—often deep differences—that can arise between that framework and the pressing, growing reality of the Federal Government's definition, installation, and enforcement of its vision of "virtues." That very government constantly strives to regulate behaviors and exercise power well beyond what is reasonable. The result could well be virtue cram-downs that are very contrary to a classic Christian understanding of a life devoted to God.

So, with that eventuality, *rendering to God and rendering to Caesar may well come into conflict with what the Federal Government desires.*

Whether maneuvering in response to the aggressive Secular Theocracy or working directly to reclaim virtue locally in American life, living a classic Christian life in America will surely take a very determined yet civil and respectful effort.

Render carefully yet boldly.

And, be of good cheer. The best is yet to come.

APPENDIX

Selected Quotes, Arranged by Theme, from
Freedom Nationally, Virtue Locally—or Socialism

A number of key themes are interwoven throughout the narrative in *Freedom Nationally, Virtue Locally—or Socialism.* Selected quotes that assist in summarizing certain key themes of the book are included below.

The key themes or topics are, in order of presentation:

★ America's Caesar

★ Virtue

★ Virtue Cram-Downs

★ Freedom and Virtue

★ Social Justice

★ Secular Theocracy

★ The Church of State

★ Contrasting Different Types of Justice

★ The Haman Strategy

★ Socialism

★ Rendering to Caesar, Rendering to God

America's Caesar

One of the most famous teachings of Jesus Christ is to render to Caesar the things that are Caesar's, and to God the things that are God's. But, first things first. The actual question faced by Americans on July 5, 1776—the morning after the Declaration of Independence—and the years immediately following was, just who is "Caesar"? (45)

The fifteen years of real-world experience between 1776 and 1791 without an effective Caesar were essential to the forging of the American understanding of Caesar in America. (46)

So, the Framers of the Constitution decided on just who "Caesar" is in America. Caesar is the people, bound by a covenant of their own making, capturing these key understandings. *In America, Caesar is "the people, bound by the Constitution."* Not just "the people." No, Caesar is the people, bound by the Constitution. (47–48)

In America, Caesar is *not* a king. In America, Caesar is *not* the often-cited, default answer of "the Federal Government." In America, Caesar *is* the people, bound by the Constitution. (48)

The long history of just who Caesar is was profoundly inverted in America in 1791. (50)

Will Americans' virtues ultimately be in the hands of the legitimate American Caesar, "the people, bound by the Constitution"? Or is Caesar, now, just "the Federal Government"? In other words, will a large number of American people continue to agree with the trend that the Federal Government can impose its virtuous notions on the entire citizenry? (69)

The [first] doctrine [of the Secular Theocracy is] that "the Federal Government is virtue-Caesar, defining and enforcing the nation's virtues." Top-down power always ultimately resides with a Federal Government. Why go to the hard work of persuading stubborn, ignorant citizens, one-by-one, of the right thing to do for social priorities, when Washingtonians who are the best and the brightest can define brand-new virtues and then actually require everyone to be virtuous? "Federal Government as virtue-Caesar" is by far the most efficient path to a virtuous society, a fair society, a society of equal outcomes. President Lyndon Johnson had it right: a Great Society is courtesy of the Federal Government. (87–88)

Jesus instructed Christians to render to Caesar. And the Framers of the U.S. Constitution essentially defined Caesar in America as "the people, bound by the Constitution." And that Constitution quite properly reserved virtues to the people, not to the Federal Government, even while delegating the job of virtuously preserving freedom to the Federal Government. (147)

Virtue

The highly conceited presumption is that the President and Congress know virtue better than ordinary Americans. So, they are ready not just to instruct Americans about virtue, they are actually going to force every American to be virtuous. (18)

Secularists may call them "values," Christians may call them "virtues," and each group thinks its belief set is superior to the other's. But whatever they are called, these are the deep passions of the politically-engaged. Some are high-minded passions, some very much less so—whichever they are, they are driving the current political scene in America.

Regardless of the label, these passions simply *must* be fulfilled, you see, because the entire country supposedly would be better off. This is the rising secular theocracy, where those in power in the gargantuan Federal Government horse-trade their way to codifying into law and enforcing every "virtue" imaginable—and many "virtues" unimaginable.

So, why aim small, at families, or communities, or churches, where true and accurate common interest can be locally determined? Why simply work to improve local organizations when the entire country could be so deeply "virtuous" in so many ways? You know: "virtue," a particular rule that you want 300 million people to obey, and fund with their own hard-earned money. (20)

So, numerous, influential Washington-attracted individuals work to fulfill their destiny of creating a Totally Virtuous America. They are busy as beavers, constantly cramming-down new virtues and installing more new requirements, in order to serve their special-interest-of-vital-importance-today-that-we-must-not-neglect.

Each time, it's just a small "virtue" needed, you see. But that "virtue" is vastly important to the future of the world, or to the animal kingdom, or to a financially-contributing constituent, or to a future employer, or even to Western civilization or its recent replacement, multiculturalism. And, every "virtue" is important enough to force every American to comply with new Federal rules, of course. (22–23)

To the contrary, real virtue is clear. Real virtue comes as a clarion call of clear-sighted conscience and conviction to individuals, not from a group-grope of literally hundreds of politicians [in the U.S. Congress]. These politicians, some of whom are quite ethically-challenged anyway, are focused on securing compromises in order to pass legislation, getting reelected every election cycle, serving very dissimilar constituents, and pleasing self-interested financial supporters. (24)

However, what much of the Bill of Rights was all about was protecting Americans from their own government expanding its power beyond handling traditional crimes into the area of personal beliefs or virtues. (51)

Freedom for Americans *to* live life as they choose, without the Federal Government coercing what religious virtues or secular virtues Americans are to live by—in other words, government that doesn't cram-down national "virtues" to individuals and local communities. (56)

Beyond that, Americans retain the right to determine their own virtues, opinions, beliefs, and actions. It is *not* the purview of the Federal Government to define and enforce the virtues of Americans. (63)

Will Americans' virtues ultimately be in the hands of the legitimate American Caesar, "the people, bound by the Constitution"? Or is Caesar, now, just "the Federal Government"? In other words, will a large number of American people continue to agree with the trend that the Federal Government can impose its virtuous notions on the entire citizenry? (69)

The question is, of course, whose virtue? "Virtue locally" is the prudently best answer, of course. It has been the best answer for over three hundred years in America. The people in Berkeley and Boulder, Dallas and Des Moines, Lancaster County and Las Vegas have established local community values, as the U.S. Constitution allows. The virtues of each local populace—however lacking or laudable to others—have historically prevailed. (69–70)

The very nature of a Federal Government program funding virtues means that *those in Congress passing the virtue legislation do not believe that the American people are better stewards of their own money and better discerners of virtue than the Federal Government is.* (80)

But, of course, the reality is that the Federal Government only *lowers* the standards and vulgarizes the virtues of a people already inclined to pursue traditional virtue. The late U.S. Senator Patrick Moynihan of New York coined a clever phrase that describes when a society starts accepting lower standards and creates new, lower norms: "defining deviancy down." (98)

Virtue is a local issue. Freedom is a national issue. (122)

Virtue is the privilege of individuals, families, churches, and communities. Basically, individuals, plus what English statesman and philosopher Edmund Burke called "little platoons." Bottom-up. Self-governing. (123)

No virtues to be introduced and enforced at the Federal level, thanks. (132)

Freedom nationally, virtue locally is the only way for virtue to be truly renewed, as the American people properly pursue their high calling: virtue. (144)

Virtue Cram-Downs

The Federal virtue-cram-down machine spoke from the mountaintop. The new law will be applied to individuals in significantly different circumstances in every nook and cranny of a very large and complex nation. Every adult American *will* purchase health coverage. (18)

The reality is crystal clear to millions of Americans on the receiving end of countless Federal virtue cram-downs. Americans are routinely losing their basic freedoms. Ironically, they are losing these freedoms to the unchecked whims and wishes of the very people they are paying to serve them. (19)

These virtue cram-downs are often led by individuals sworn to uphold the U.S. Constitution. Apparently, however, these people are not always focused on whether their actions are Constitutional. Instead, they are primarily focused on "improving" the lives of Americans by their compliance to brand new "virtues." And with every Federal virtue cram-down, freedom is reduced. (22)

So, no new Federal virtue cram-downs. From the left or from the right. Period. (132)

All the while, the Christian must vigilantly understand the differences—often deep differences—that can arise between that framework and the pressing, growing reality of the Federal Government's definition, installation, and enforcement of its vision of "virtues." That very government constantly strives to regulate behaviors and exercise power well beyond what is reasonable. The result could well be virtue cram-downs that are very contrary to a classic Christian understanding of a life devoted to God. (148)

Freedom and Virtue

When Americans ask the Federal Government to deliver both freedom and virtue, they will ultimately get neither. (24)

In a modern representative government, the only antidote to the Secular Theocracy, the Church of State, and the end result of virtue-socialism and economic-socialism is "freedom nationally, virtue locally." And it's been there all along. (98)

Americans are right to want freedom in America. And Americans are right to want virtue in America. It's just that any strategies short of "freedom nationally, virtue locally" are, sooner or later, fatally flawed. The Secular Theocrats will simply take over. That's the fruit of their relentless efforts to create a freedom-crippling Totally Virtuous America. (141)

The only clear path to America's greatness is "freedom nationally, virtue locally." Freedom nationally, virtue locally is the only way freedom will be truly preserved, as the Federal Government properly, and virtuously, pursues its high calling: freedom. Freedom nationally, virtue locally is the only way for virtue to be truly renewed, as the American people properly pursue their high calling: virtue. (144)

Social Justice

When a community reaches out and supports the needy in their community, that's true American virtue at work! In fact, that actually happens countless times every day in America, via voluntary outreaches and ministries providing food, clothing, medical services, job training, and much more.

And, if a community such as New York City or San Francisco further wants to tax its residents or visitors—sometimes quite heavily—to fund its social priorities, then well done, generous citizens! Over time, the residents who don't like that priority can change either their address or modify their city's policies via future elections.

In all cases, local people—not cloistered Federal employees spending taxpayer money—are best qualified to assess the validity and depth of the needs in their community and can make adjustments in funding and services more easily and quickly. (83)

Institutionalization of covetousness and greed, in the name of social justice? Is it "justice" to institutionalize covetousness and greed in recipients of Federal Government largesse, putting them in a very real bondage to the Federal Government? Is it courageous? Is it statesmanship?

And all this is done in the name of virtue.

No. There's a better way. There is a way with more direct accountability, personally and politically, for both politicians and their constituents. And that way is to address the needs of the truly poor at the personal level, the community level, or the state level. All these levels of help eventually have to pay their own bills. (84)

. . . phrases such as "social justice" work very well [for the Secular Theocracy], because nobody can really define social justice. And a definition of "social justice" is not even wanted—because that would limit the vast number of times that the Secular Theocracy can call for social justice and indict the entire society for its neglect of the Secular Theocracy agenda. (88)

The Secular Theocracy's social justice demands that Americans love their Neighbors, but that isn't the end of the story: citizens must love their Neighbors exactly however the Federal Government instructs them. (92)

Far from ignorant about conditions both in the U.S. and internationally, these Christians have a very formidable understanding, a broad understanding, a real-world-experience understanding of *genuine, directly-accountable-to-funders, non-politicized social justice*—one that eclipses that of the Church of State and is getting increasingly difficult for the Church of State to defeat. (110)

With this strategy, the Church of State in America has been winning practically everything it desires for its *Federal-Government-controlled, always-defined-for-political-advantage, lack-of-true-accountability "social justice"* and for changed individual behaviors in the name of environmentalism. To pretend otherwise is an exercise in self-deception. (121)

During His earthly ministry, Jesus Christ never coerced a single person into belief or action. He didn't coerce others in the name of social justice, and He didn't coerce others in the name of virtue. Jesus didn't even coerce people to believe in Him. (132–133)

A number of Christians across the political spectrum kinda-pretty-much hate to admit it, but they *want* the Federal Government to force their version of the Christian thing on others, whatever "the Christian thing" is for them. Is it compassion, or social justice, or universal health care, or better behavior? Their hope is in the Federal Government to bolster, or leverage, or perhaps even supplant the Church's mission—whatever they perceive that to be, whether liberal or conservative.

And authentic Christianity is the loser. That's because coercive Christianity isn't authentic Christianity at all. And when coercive Christianity is sponsored via the Federal Government in the form of taxpayer-funded social justice programs or religious rules, non-Christians *and even many Christians* can mistakenly start believing that merely good works or following rules for good behavior represent the authentic, full practice of the Christian faith. That is a deeply inadequate rendering of the Good News of Jesus Christ. (134)

Secular Theocracy

This is the rising secular theocracy, where those in power in the gargantuan Federal Government horse-trade their way to codifying into law and enforcing every "virtue" imaginable—and many "virtues" unimaginable. (20)

The problem is, a number of key Americans, at least those with preferred parking in Washington, DC, are *routinely revealing by their rhetoric, and by their actions, that they do want a Secular Theocracy.* You know, a theocracy, a "national community" with religious-like, Federally-enforced laws and regulations that everybody *will* follow to supposedly make the entire nation virtuous. But this theocracy is run by a relatively few people *using Secular standards*, without the "God" part that so many simple-minded Americans are clinging to, you know. (87)

A system of "never enough" must also have indulgences, so that the behavior of the favored elite can be rationalized away, and so that the Secular Theocracy's key supporters can be rewarded by ignoring their Secular sins, even while their peers are held accountable. (90–91)

Of course, the Secular Theocracy has obstacles. Say a U.S. taxpayer makes plans to spend his personal funds to help the Mexican citizen south of the border. And he does not want to send that very money to Washington to fund the health care of the Mexican citizen living illegally in the United States. Well, that taxpayer is racist. Why? Because the doctrine of mushy terminology rules: "racist" is whatever the Secular Theocracy says it is to suit its purposes of the moment, time and again. (91)

The Secular Theocracy's social justice demands that Americans love their Neighbors, but that isn't the end of the story: citizens must love their Neighbors exactly however the Federal Government instructs them. Some of the Federal Government's "instruction" is financial, such as higher taxes on all citizens, with the resulting financial distribution targeted to helping-the-Secular-Theocracy Neighbors. Some of the Federal Government's "instruction" is behavioral. Just who will Americans associate with, and where? The Secular Theocracy will instruct Americans, and all of the instructions are mandatory. Penalties will be severe. (92)

"Secular" definitely doesn't mean neutral. "Secular" must defeat all competitors for the hearts and minds of a critical mass of key voting constituencies and campaign funders. This control only comes with all of the preceding doctrines being in play. The Secular Theocracy is especially not-neutral towards the Christian faith—unless or until Christians submit to the policies and power of the Secular Theocracy. (93)

Of course, the Secular Theocrat would likely say that the leveling of virtues is a leveling "up," a betterment of virtues, according to their clearly superior beliefs. And so we return to the romanticized notion of the Secular Theocracy that the Federal Government can actually define virtues and then deliver virtues, all for the supposed betterment of an entire nation. This system is being installed every day in America, ever more deeply. (98)

The George W. Bush Administration followed the Secular Theocracy playbook perfectly in its rhetoric about "compassionate conservatism" and in some of its policies. Prime policy examples were its well-meaning No Child Left Behind Federal-nannyism in education, its policy of increasing the percentage of low-income loans mandated in Fannie Mae and Freddie Mac portfolios,[27] and its newly-formed White

House Office of Faith-Based and Community Initiatives (now operating under different management, values, and labeling, *of course*).

With such policies, the Bush Administration *inappropriately* affirmed many Americans' expectations that the Federal Government should be in the virtue business. And they did this from a supposedly politically-conservative position. Since those types of policies expand the Federal Government's programs and power, the Secular Theocracy will simply take over and once again increase the Federal Government's power to "improve" the nation's "social justice." (103)

The Secular Theocracy routinely uses its doctrines, moralizing language, and ever-creeping legislation to manipulate and control huge portions of Americans' personal behavior. To all appearances, that is working well and is well-poised for continued success with regard to environmental issues. And many Christians are allowing, and in some cases even promoting, the mushy terminology of creation care to be a key driving wedge for this Secular Theocratic success. (119)

The Church of State has found the soft underbelly of American Christianity and will keep plugging away. The Secular Theocrats have identified key issues that have varying degrees of Biblical plausibility and applicability, such as environmental and social issues. Then, no matter the true level of legitimacy, they dress up those pigs to be never-enough-done-for-them dire needs, needs that presumably *only* the Federal Government and the governments of the world can address. (121)

Whether maneuvering in response to the aggressive Secular Theocracy or working directly to reclaim virtue locally in American life, living a classic Christian life in America will surely take a very determined yet civil and respectful effort. (148)

The Church of State

Why is the Secular-Theocratic Federal Government fittingly labeled the "national-virtue-defining-and-enforcing Church of State?" Well, because the "Church" role *presumptively defines* "national virtue," while the "State" role *vigorously enforces* "national virtue." And the full power of the State is behind the penalty-laden enforcement of the Church of State's numerous laws and voluminous regulations.

Having your organization, the Church of State, control both the definition and the legal enforcement of virtues is *very* convenient and tidy. That is surely gratifying to every would-be King George in every nook and cranny of the Federal Government. Pity the poor Churches outside the State that have to rely merely on moral persuasion. (96)

They [some Americans] are relieved, even overjoyed, that the Federal Government is taking care of it all. Simply write one check to the Church of State every year, if you pay income taxes. If you don't, well, that's OK, brother, because the Church of State knows you are a hapless, financially-strapped victim of capitalist oppressors, such as the pizza parlor owner with her business located in the strip mall just down the street. (97)

But what the Church of State doggedly pursues is really both economic-socialism *and* virtue-socialism. The two goals are to force the leveling of wealth through the government's redistribution of private resources (economic-socialism) *and* to force the leveling of virtues by government laws and extensive regulation of behavior (virtue-socialism). (97–98)

The modern Church of State is where elitist Federal Government employees define, then institutionalize, "virtue" for millions of Americans, and reduce their freedoms in the bargain. In the battle for defining and delivering virtues, the Church of State has made a virtual art form of co-opting certain Christians and defeating other Christians. (99)

These two desires, to maintain a Christian nation and to create a righteous nation, have worked to entice a number of Christians to focus on and engage in Federal virtue-politics. These Christians take the bait and self-defeatingly respond to the Church of State whenever it pushes national virtue-politics to the forefront of the public agenda. The Church of State does this, unrelentingly, in order to feed its omnivorous appetite for power, control, and beholden constituents. (101)

The more that American Christians (or any Americans, for that matter) engage in Federal virtue-politics—top-down—the more they follow the playbook of the Secular Theocrats running the Church of State. The Secular Theocrats actually want the Christians to talk virtue-talk and to set up political virtue-platforms nationally. (102)

Similar to Haman and his strategy, the Christians pursuing virtue via Federal policies are simply over their heads strategically. They sincerely desire virtue for the nation, use virtue language (instead of simply using freedom language) in their national political discourse, and are happy whenever they win individual battles at the Federal level. But what they don't factor in is that only the Church of State is the ultimate winner when Christians engage in Federal virtue-politics.

The Church of State is actually well-served when Christians win some Federal virtue-politics battles. These battles are often ones that many American Christians would not support at all without a specific or implied Christian label, such as the creation of the White House Office of Faith-Based and Community Initiatives. In this way, the Church of State may be granted more wins as part of the political horse-trading of "Federal virtues" in play. Or, the Church of State may expect to simply convert Christians' supposed wins over to the Church of State's win column later. Sometimes, both tactics may be working simultaneously. (104–105)

But those developments are never enough for the Secular Theocrats, of course. So when the rhetoric heats up, these wealth distribution realities are treated as if they never happened. Why do Secular Theocrats actually act as if the iPod-as-a-common-luxury world of today is the same as the horse-and-buggy era? That happens because the Church of State was left out of the action as the required middleman and therefore missed the opportunity to create ever-more-beholden constituents of the Federal Government. When multimillionaire professional athletes negotiate their service contracts with the billionaire professional team owners in America, the Church of State will *still* find victims. (116)

Will large numbers of American Christians soon spend more time devotedly recycling each week ("Jesus as soda-can recycler") than in sharing their faith in Jesus as Savior of souls? How many Christians are already doing so? The Secular Theocrats are surely pleased with the fast-growing submission of targeted Christians to an agenda that the Church of State defines, controls, and enforces. (120–121)

"Freedom nationally, virtue locally" is the strategy to deploy against the pretensions and coercive activity of the Church of State. (121)

Christianity simply will not succeed in making the culture either Christian or righteous because Christians or the Church strongly align top-down with the Federal power structure in a modern representative government. The modern, representative-government Church of State is actually a direct, fierce, cunning, monopolistic, and unrelenting competitor to the Church founded two thousand years ago. *That's why the day that the Christian Church starts relying substantially on the modern, representative-based Federal Government to instill or affirm Christian truths and to create or sustain Christian culture is the day that substantive Christianity starts to decline.*

Any rock-solid progress in making Christianity truly work is accomplished bottom-up and then renewed in local social structures, generation after generation—*that's how both the making of Christian disciples and social conservatism actually succeed.*(133)

All freedom-focused Americans must pull together in a coalition to defeat top-down "virtues" coerced by those politicians and bureaucrats from the national-virtue-defining-and-enforcing Church of State. (141)

Contrasting Different Types of Justice

The Federal Government's irreplaceable role is to preserve Americans' freedom. That includes the proper handling of traditional crimes against persons and property (traditional justice) and the ensuring of equal access of all citizens to public accommodations (freedom-based justice). But the Federal Government should not be in the virtue business. Besides, the Federal Government is not competent at defining virtue, and it is not competent at delivering virtue. (80)

Straightforward, accountable definitions simply don't work to get the results desired [by the Secular Theocracy]. Terms such as "justice" won't do, because that means a particular person took a particular action that was clearly wrong by objective, clearly defined, and written-down standards.

Instead, phrases such as "social justice" work very well, because nobody can really define social justice. And a definition of "social justice" is not even wanted—because that would limit the vast number of times that the Secular Theocracy can call for social justice and indict the entire society for its neglect of the Secular Theocracy agenda.

However, it is vitally important to use the word "justice" within the full phrase; this works to condemn the people who are not moved to do *something—something really, really important, urgent, and necessary*—as conveniently defined by those in the Secular Theocracy. After all, "justice" demands it.

The trick is to always blur "social justice" with both traditional justice (addressing traditional crimes against persons and property) and freedom-based justice (e.g., equal access to public accommodations) in discussions, debates, speeches, and publications. This works to presume that social justice is of the same importance and on the same, or even higher, moral plane as traditional justice and freedom-based justice. (88–89)

The Secular Theocracy's social justice demands that Americans love their Neighbors, but that isn't the end of the story: citizens must love their Neighbors exactly however the Federal Government instructs them. (92)

No virtues to be introduced and enforced at the Federal level, thanks. That includes those newly discovered virtues politically positioned in the name of freedom-based justice. In reality, that's the forcing of *new* or *revised* social conventions, coupled with the expectation of de facto special accommodations by an often widely unwilling citizenry. And that's done using the top-down power of the Federal Government. Rather, freedom-based justice essentially corrects circumstances where the unjustly-unenfranchised are not permitted to fully participate in an *established*, citizen-participation-in-public-citizenship act (e.g., voting, access to public accommodations) solely because of their ethnicity or original-equipment gender. (132)

The Haman Strategy

Here's the story of Haman. In the Old Testament Book about Esther in the Bible, Haman was the King's right-hand man. Haman hated Jews. Haman built gallows explicitly for the hanging of the innocent Jewish leader Mordecai. But the king, husband of the Jew Esther, ultimately hanged Haman on his own gallows.

So, here's the Haman Strategy. Haman planned how others would conform to his wishes, overestimated his power and its sustainability in the political process, devised his strategy without due regard for the actions and reactions of key political players, and had his very designs for others ultimately used against him.

Haman was evil. And authentic Christians are not evil.

But similar to Haman and his strategy, the Christians pursuing virtue via Federal policies are simply over their heads strategically. They sincerely desire virtue for the nation, use virtue language (instead of simply using freedom language) in their national political discourse, and are happy whenever they win individual battles at the Federal level. But what they don't factor in is that only the Church of State is the ultimate winner when Christians engage in Federal virtue-politics. (104)

Christians' Haman Strategy simply results in self-inflicted defeat. (107)

Americans should not take the bait of playing Federal virtue-politics. Christians should not be pursuing Federal virtue initiatives, as their good intentions are absorbed into the Secular Theocracy's programs and processes in order to achieve its own, different ends. So, Christians should shed the suicidal Haman Strategy. Virtue is a local issue. Freedom is a national issue. If Americans shed the Haman Strategy, a national freedom coalition can win the day and create the opportunity for freedom nationally and virtue locally. That restores both freedom and virtue to the rightful owners. (122)

This is not about disparaging the intent of well-meaning people to instill timeless virtues in the nation. It's about which strategy works, and specifically the failure of any currently-seductive, top-down strategy of Christians—a Haman Strategy—to restore the culture. (139)

Socialism

These [Federal Government] agendas are really just socialism. But they are two types of socialism, both "economic-socialism," where the goal is the redistribution of wealth by the government, and "virtue-socialism," where the goal is to ratchet the entire country's behavior to a deadly serious political-correctness in all areas of culture and life. That political correctness was originally interpreted as harmless foolishness by many Americans, but it's a grim business now. The Federal Government's wealth redistribution and cram-down of secular "virtues" in America is being accomplished by force of law and regulation. (12)

Socialism has pretty much historically been considered an economic philosophy or system: a Federal Government controlling the means of production and leveling the economic results for people. But what the Church of State doggedly pursues is really both economic-socialism *and* virtue-socialism. The two goals are to force the leveling of wealth through the government's redistribution of private resources (economic-socialism) *and* to force the leveling of virtues by government laws and extensive regulation of behavior (virtue-socialism). (97–98)

. . . freedom nationally, virtue locally is the only way to defeat the virtue-socialism and economic-socialism being forcibly crammed-down by Washington onto the rest of the country. (144)

Rendering to Caesar, Rendering to God

But, since the Constitution's Bill of Rights reserves virtues to the people, *rendering to Caesar Constitutionally* means handling virtues locally, through individuals, families, houses of worship, and local communities—even when citizens disagree with the virtues that other Americans select.

And, since the Constitution's Bill of Rights reserves virtues to the people, *rendering to Caesar Christianly* means the Christian is personally accountable to God for virtues and proper stewardship in those very same local vehicles. (148)

So, with that eventuality [of the Federal Government defining and enforcing Americans' personal virtues], *rendering to God and rendering to Caesar may well come into conflict with what the Federal Government desires.* (148)

Render carefully yet boldly. (148)

ENDNOTES

1 Sidney and Beatrice Webb, *Soviet Communism: A New Civilization?* (New York: Charles Scribner's Sons, 1938), 1036.

2 Colin Sullivan, "Calif. water agency changes course on delta smelt," *New York Times*, May 12, 2009, http://www.nytimes.com/gwire/2009/05/12/12greenwire-calif-water-agency-changes-course-on-delta-sme-10572.html.

3 John Ellis, "Both sides claim victory in water compromise," *The Fresno Bee*, June 23, 2010, http://www.fresnobee.com/2010/06/23/1982263/both-sides-claim-victory-in-water.html#storylink=misearch

4 Kate Andersen Brower, "Obama Defends His Health-Care Plan as 'Right Thing to Do'," *Business Week*, March 17, 2010, http://www.businessweek.com/news/2010-03-17/obama-defends-his-health-care-plan-as-right-thing-to-do-.html.

5 Thomas Jefferson to William Charles Jarvis, 28 September 1820, The Thomas Jefferson Papers Series 1. General Correspondence. 1651-1827, Library of Congress.

6 Forrest McDonald, *Recovering the Past: A Historian's Memoir* (Lawrence, KS: University Press of Kansas, 2004), 183-184.

7 Thomas Jefferson, *Notes on the State of Virginia*, ed. Frank Shuffelton (New York: Penguin Books, 1999), 126.

8 "We are at war," *The Patriot*, directed by Roland Emmerich (2000; Culver City, CA: Columbia TriStar Home Video, 2000), DVD.

9 H. W. Brands, *The First American: The Life and Times of Benjamin Franklin* (New York: Doubleday, 2000), 716.

10 The Virginia Declaration of Rights, The Charters of Freedom, National Archives, accessed August 24, 2010, archives.gov/exhibits/charters/virginia_declaration_of_rights.html

11 John Jay, "Charge to the Grand Jury of Ulster County (1777)." With an introduction by Jerod Patterson, The John Jay Institute, accessed August 24, 2010, http://www.johnjayinstitute.org/index.cfm?get=get.paper_12292006

12 Confucius, *The Chinese Classics, Volume 1, Confucian Analects*, trans. James Legge (Memphis, TN: General Books, 2010), 21.

13 U.S. Const. amend. IX.

14 U.S. Const. amend. X.

15 U.S. Const. amend. I.

16 Frederick Douglass, *Narrative of the Life of Frederick Douglass: An American Slave and Other Writings* (New York: Fall River Press, 2010), 161.

17 Chief Standing Bear's Speech. *The Indian Journal*, Timeless Truths Free Online Library, accessed August 24, 2010, library.timelesstruths.org/texts/Stories_Worth_Rereading/Standing_Bears_Speech/

18 U.S. Const. amend. XIX.

19 Indian Affairs: Law and Treaties, vol. IV, Laws. ed. Charles J. Kappler. Government Printing Office, 1929, accessed August 24, 2010, digital.library.okstate.edu/kappler/vol4/html_files/v4p1165.html

20 Civil Rights Act (1964), National Archives and Records Administration, accessed August 24, 2010, ourdocuments.gov/doc.php?flash=old&doc=97#

21 An Act for the Suppression of Trade in, and Circulation of, obscene Literature and Articles for immoral Use, 17 Stat. 598 (1873).

22 George Orwell, *Animal Farm and 1984*. With an introduction by Christopher Hitchens (Orlando, FL: Harcourt, Inc., 2003), 80.

23 Christopher Caldwell, "Easy Credit, Hard Landing: The Financial Insights of Raghuram Rajan," *The Weekly Standard*, July 26, 2010, https://www.weeklystandard.com/articles/easy-credit-hard-landing.

24 Edmund Burke, *American Taxation, a Speech, Delivered April 19, 1774*, ed. Albert Blaisdell (New York: Maynard, Merrill, & Co., 1892), 53.

25 Richard J. Mouw, "Current Religious Thought: Abraham Kuyper: A Man for This Season" *Christianity Today*, October 26, 1998, http://www.christianitytoday.com/ct/1998/october26/8tco86.html

26 Seneca, *Epistles 66-92 (Loeb Classical Library)*, trans. Richard M. Gummere (Cambridge, MA: Harvard University Press, 1920), 285.

27 Christopher Caldwell, "Easy Credit, Hard Landing: The Financial Insights of Raghuram Rajan," *The Weekly Standard*, July 26, 2010, https://www.weeklystandard.com/articles/easy-credit-hard-landing.